The Rational Guide To

Small Office and Home Networking

PUBLISHED BY

Rational Press - An imprint of the Mann Publishing Group
710 Main Street, 6th Floor
PO Box 580
Rollinsford, NH 03869, USA
www.rationalpress.com
www.mannpublishing.com
+1 (603) 601-0325

ISBN: 0-9726888-2-X
Library of Congress Control Number (LCCN): 2005927766
Printed and bound in the United States of America.
10 9 8 7 6 5 4 3 2

Trademarks

Mann Publishing, Mann Publishing Group, Agility Press, Rational Press, Inc.Press, NetImpress, Farmhouse Press, BookMann Press, The Rational Guide To, Rational Guides, ExecuGuide, AdminExpert, From the Source, the Mann Publishing Group logo, the Agility Press logo, the Rational Press logo, the Inc.Press logo, Timely Business Books, Rational Guides for a Fast-Paced World, and Custom Corporate Publications are all trademarks or registered trademarks of Mann Publishing Incorporated.

All brand names, product names, and technologies presented in this book are trademarks or registered trademarks of their respective holders.

Disclaimer of Warranty

While the publisher and author(s) have taken care to ensure accuracy of the contents of this book, they make no representation or warranties with respect to the accuracy or completeness of the contents of this book and specifically disclaim any implied warranties of merchantability or fitness for a specific purpose. The advice, strategies, or steps contained herein may not be suitable for your situation. You should consult with a professional where appropriate before utilizing the advice, strategies, or steps contained herein. Neither the publisher nor author(s) shall be liable for any loss of profit or any other commercial damages, including but not limited to special, incidental, consequential, or other damages.

Credits

Author:	Jim Boyce
Technical Editor:	Michael Heitland
Copy Editor:	Jeff Edman
Index:	Barbara Benjamin
Book Layout:	Molly Barnaby
Series Concept:	Anthony T. Mann
Cover Concept:	Marcelo Paiva
Proofreader:	Keri Lewis

All Mann Publishing Group books may be purchased at bulk discounts.

The Rational Guide To

Small Office and Home Networking

Jim Boyce

RATIONAL PRESS

An imprint of the
www.mannpublishing.com

About the Author

Jim Boyce has authored and co-authored over 50 books on computer software, hardware, and related technologies. He is a former Contributing Editor for WINDOWS Magazine and now contributes articles frequently to Microsoft.com, TechRepublic.com, OfficeLetter. com, and other online and print publications. Jim previously co-owned and operated an Internet Service Provider business and supervised all networking issues for the company, from client network design to infrastructure development. In past lives Jim has also been a UNIX system administrator, CAD system manager, structural steel designer, and college instructor. Jim enjoys flying real and model aircraft, woodworking, and his family.

Acknowledgements

I offer my sincere appreciation to Michael Heitland of 702 Communications (www.702com. com) for his superb job of tech-editing this book. Mike provided excellent suggestions for additions and clarification. I also offer many thanks to Joe Barnett of Coopers Technology Group (www.coopersinc.com) for also reviewing the manuscript for technical accuracy. Thanks also to Bill Zumwalde of B2 Networking (www.b2site.com) for his suggestions and assistance with the book.

I also thank Tony Mann and Jeff Edman at Rational Press for the opportunity to do this book. It was my first book with Rational Press and was a positive experience from day one. Kudos also to Keri Lewis and Molly Barnaby for the great job of editing and laying out the book. Everyone's efforts have resulted in an excellent book.

I also appreciate very much Roger Phillips (www.kapowphoto.com) and Rick Anderson (www.themidweek.com) allowing me to take photos of their network installations to include in the book.

About Rational Guides

Rational Guides, from Rational Press, provide a no-nonsense approach to publishing based on both a practicality and price that make them rational. Rational Guides are compact books of fewer than 224 pages. Each Rational Guide is constructed with the highest quality writing and production materials—at an affordable price. All Rational Guides are intended to be as complete as possible within the 224-page size constraint. Furthermore, all Rational Guides come with bonus materials, such as additional chapters, applications, code, utilities, or other resources. To download these materials, just register your book at www.rationalpress.com. See the instruction page at the end of this book to find out how to register your book.

Who Should Read This Book

Setting up a home or small office network can be a daunting task the first time you do it. Even so, designing and setting up a network isn't overly difficult once you learn the basics. This book will take you through the entire process of planning, wiring, choosing network hardware, and configuring your network. With the help of a few inexpensive, commonly-available tools, you'll have your network up and running in no time!

Conventions Used In This Book

The following conventions are used throughout this book:

▶ *Italics* — First introduction of a term.

▶ **Bold** — Exact name of an item or object that appears on the computer screen, such as menus, buttons, dropdown lists, or links.

▶ `Mono-spaced text` — Used to show a Web URL address, computer language code, or expressions as you must exactly type them.

▶ **Menu1⇨Menu2** — Hierarchical Windows menus in the order you must select them.

Tech Tip:
This box gives you additional technical advice about the option, procedure, or step being explained in the chapter.

Note:
This box gives you additional information to keep in mind as you read.

FREE *Bonus:*
This box lists additional free materials or content available on the Web after you register your book at `www.rationalpress.com`.

Caution
This box alerts you to special considerations or additional advice.

Contents

Contents

Contents

Network Concepts and Planning

Chapter 1

Networking Overview

This book focuses on small office and home office (SOHO) networks and the needs of those two scenarios aren't always the same. Sure, there is a lot of overlap in terms of needs, but the wants are sometimes different. Let's take a look at the most common uses of SOHO networking.

Why Do You Need a Network?

The answer to that question might seem like a no-brainer, but when you put some thought into it, the answer might not be so obvious. Why do you need a network?

Sharing File and Printer Resources

By far the most common reason people offer for why they want a network is to share files and printers. In an office environment, users often need to share documents, templates, and other files. Sharing folders and files offers several benefits for businesses:

► **Reduce errors** — Working with a single document rather than multiple copies of that document prevents copies from becoming unsynchronized.

► **Save space** — File sharing saves storage space by eliminating multiple copies of common documents.

► **Support collaboration** — It's easy to collaborate on documents when you can share those documents, and a network often provides the most effective means for sharing documents.

▶ **Simplify data backup** — Users are notoriously bad about backing up their data, even if they have the means to do so. Place critical documents on a server to enable an administrator to ensure that the documents are backed up on a regular basis.

▶ **Provide data security** — Hosting documents and other files on a server gives a network administrator control over who has access to those files. Although you can exercise some control over workstation sharing security, you have complete control over server security and therefore complete control over file sharing and access.

Home users can also benefit from file sharing. Some of the benefits are the same, although for somewhat different reasons. For example, as photography has trended from film to digital, it has become common for home users to store their digital photos on a computer. You can share those photos from a single computer to make them accessible to everyone without duplicating them or wasting disk space. Likewise, you can share music files and other documents with a home network.

Printers are another common reason to use a network. Today, printers are relatively inexpensive, so it's not cost prohibitive for every user to have a printer. But when you take into account the relatively high cost of consumables such as printer cartridges, putting a printer on every desk just doesn't make as much sense. Centralizing printing on the network offers a couple of advantages:

▶ **Cost savings** — Fewer printers mean lower costs for printers and consumables. You also reduce support costs.

▶ **Conserve desktop space** — Let's face it, most people have too much stuff on their desks already. Centralize printers where possible to unclutter the office.

▶ **Control printer access** — Controlling who can print to a printer and when are important factors for both business and home networks.

Sharing an Internet Connection

In the early days of networking, file and printer sharing was by far the most common reason to install a network. Today, sharing an Internet connection could be considered more important by many people, particularly home users.

Internet access has become such an important part of many businesses that Internet availability ranks close to electricity and heat in importance. Users need to send and receive e-mail, share documents, do research, and much more, all of which relies on the Internet. A lot of companies effectively grind to a halt today when their Internet service or e-mail server goes down. Reliable, shared Internet access is a must-have for many businesses, particularly small businesses that need every advantage to compete in today's market.

For home users, shared Internet access is much more a convenience than a necessity. Having owned an ISP, however, I can tell you that most home users don't see it that way— it's as critical as power and running water to many, and even more important than that to some. Whether you check your e-mail once a day or spend hours on the Net, you probably don't want to wait for someone else to finish using the computer so you can surf. See Chapter 2 to learn more about network speed as it relates to Internet access.

Convenience

Beyond the benefits of file sharing, printer sharing, and Internet access are the less tangible benefits offered by a network. Those benefits and their importance depend in large part on how you use your network and your computers, but I'd hazard a guess that wireless access is probably the most important of them.

If you have a notebook computer, it's great to be able to work anywhere in your office or your home. With a wireless network in place, you can access files on other computers, print, browse the Internet, and check your e-mail, all from the relative comfort of the conference room, sofa, or deck. If you have a Tablet PC with wireless access at home, I'll bet sooner or later you'll find yourself browsing the Internet from the comfort of your bed!

Wired networks also offer convenience, whether at the office or at home. You don't have to make the trek upstairs or across the building to another computer to grab a file. You don't have to copy a file to a computer with a printer to print the document. Perhaps more important, you won't have to kick a coworker or one of your children (or worse, your spouse) off of a computer so you can check your e-mail!

What Have We Missed?

While the reasons for having a network that I've already mentioned are certainly important ones, they aren't the only ones. Adding a network opens up other possibilities, as well.

For example, with a network in place, you can install and use certain server-based applications (other than file and printer sharing) that are not possible without a network. You might install your own e-mail server, for example, or set up a shared database to allow multiple users to track inventory, sales, or other information in real time. Microsoft Outlook users can share their contacts and other data across a network, either with or without Microsoft's Exchange Server as a back-end mail server. Bookkeepers can share a single set of books across the network. Designers can share parts libraries and other data.

In the home, a network can mean more fun. For example, you can play multiplayer games with others in your home or across the Internet (or both). You can also stream music from hundreds of Internet radio stations to your home stereo.

Whatever plans you have for your network today will likely change—at least some—as you build the network, begin to use it, and become more comfortable with it. As you start the planning stages, think about all of the ways you use your computer now and take into account how things would be different or better with a network in place. If you're installing a network for your business, take the time to examine all of your business practices in light of the network. In many cases, installing a network is simply the first step in a major shift in the way you will do business. If you understand at the outset how you will come to use the network over time, you'll be better equipped to design the network for tomorrow's needs as well as today's.

Networking Options

Not too many years ago, the options for building a small network were very limited. Today, you have plenty of options! Often, the best solution merges multiple options into a single virtual network. Chapter 2 offers a more in-depth look at these options, but I include them here to help you begin to think about which is the best match for your needs and your technical capabilities. Before we get started, however, let's get you familiar with a few terms.

Terms to Know

Like any other computer field, networking is full of jargon. There are some terms you should know as you begin learning about and planning for a network.

► **Gateway** — A device that serves as a connecting device between two networks; in a small network, the term gateway typically refers to the connection between a private network and the Internet.

► **Broadband** — A transmission method that allows for multiple communications paths, typically used for high-speed connection to the Internet such as a Digital Subscriber Line (DSL) or cable connection, but can include satellite connections.

► **Hub** — A device that connects one or more computers or other devices to a network; typically less expensive than switches but provide lesser performance (see Chapter 3).

► **Network Interface Card (NIC) a.k.a. Network Adapter** — A device installed in or connected to a device (typically a computer) that connects that device to the network.

► **Node** — Any device on the network.

► **Packet** — A collection of data that is transmitted on a network.

► **Protocol** — The communications method that devices (nodes) on the network use to communicate with one another. TCP/IP is today's most commonly used protocol suite.

► **Router** — A device that routes network packets from one network segment to another, such as from a private network to the Internet (and vice-versa).

► **Server** — A device, typically a computer, that provides some service (such as file or print sharing) to other devices.

► **Switch** — A device that connects one or more computers to a network.

► **Wireless Access Point (WAP)** — A device that provides access to a network through a wireless connection.

► **Workstation** — A computer that is used primarily for end-user functions such as running applications; workstations can also perform server functions.

Wired Networks

Today it seems that wireless access has been around forever, but it wasn't too long ago that wired networks were the only option. Even so, a wired network still makes sense for many businesses, and to a lesser degree, homes. See Chapter 2 to learn about the advantages and disadvantages of wired versus wireless.

In a wired network, networking cables connect computers and other devices on the network. The most commonly used type of cable today is called Category 5, or Cat5, which contains four pairs of wires. The actual conductors are individually insulated, thin copper wires. Each pair is twisted to reduce crosstalk (interference from other pairs or other cables).

Tech Tip:
Cat5e cable will support 1Gbps networks and is a good choice if you want to ensure maximum network speed now and for the future. Choose Cat6 for growth to 10Gbps networks. See Chapter 2 to learn more.

In a typical wired network, hubs or switches serve as distribution points for the network. Each computer connects to a hub or switch, and the hub/switch connects to other hubs/ switches to enable the network to branch to other rooms, other floors, or even other buildings. Different wired network *topologies* exist, each offering certain benefits. See Chapter 2 to learn more about network topology. *Topology* refers to the way in which devices are interconnected on the network.

In a nutshell, wired networks offer the best performance in terms of raw speed and throughput. As you'll learn in Chapter 9, wired networks are more secure than wireless networks—another advantage. However, wired networks take more work to install than wireless networks.

Wireless Networks

Although wireless networking technology has been available for several years, inexpensive wireless networking devices are relatively new and getting cheaper almost by the day. With improvements in security, speed, and range, wireless has become a great choice for small and home office networks.

In a typical wireless network, wireless access points serve to connect wireless devices to a network. Often, the access point is connected to a wired broadband connection to provide Internet access for the wireless devices. Also, the access point often includes a built-in switch to enable wired devices to connect through the access point to the network.

Powerline Networking

If wiring a network isn't something you want to tackle and wireless solutions don't fit the bill, an attractive alternative is *powerline networking*. This networking scheme uses the electrical wiring in your house or business in place of network cabling. So, you can locate a network device anywhere there is an electrical outlet.

Powerline networking offers the significant advantage of not requiring any additional wiring labor, although performance is less than a traditional wired network (roughly 3Mbps versus 100Mbps). However, a powerline network provides faster throughput than a broadband connection, so if Internet browsing is the main use for your network, powerline could be a good choice. See Chapter 2 for a more detailed discussion of the pros and cons of powerline networking.

Power-Over-Ethernet (PoE)

It isn't always practical to run power to a device because of the device's distance from an established power source, the building's structure, or the lack of capacity for additional circuits in the building's distribution panel.

A possible solution to these scenarios is *power-over-ethernet*, or PoE. PoE uses special equipment to inject power into twisted pair LAN cables. At the remote end of the cable, a remote device takes its power from the LAN cable. Because the network doesn't require all four pairs of wire for data, a pair is available for power. PoE can be a very useful addition to your network, but will require some additional equipment to implement. See Chapter 2 for a more detailed discussion of PoE.

Client/Server Versus Peer-to-Peer Networks

There is another issue to consider before you begin planning and implementing your network. Will you implement a server-based, a peer-to-peer network, or a combination of the two?

In a *server-based network*, all network resources are shared by one or more designated servers. Typically, the server handles logon and authentication services for the network to secure those resources. In a *peer-to-peer network*, each workstation or other device on the network can share its resources with others.

In general, a server-based network offers much better security than a peer-to-peer network. You can control resource access with user accounts that are centrally located on the server, which also simplifies security management.

In small business networks that don't require extensive resource sharing or multiple levels of security, a server operating system such as Windows Server can be overkill. In these simple networks, Windows XP Professional can be a very workable and less expensive alternative. You can still host all of the shared resources from a single Windows XP computer, which means only one set of user accounts to manage on that computer. What you lose by moving from Windows Server to Windows XP is the capability to use centralized security to secure resources elsewhere on the network and a limit of no more than ten concurrent connections to the server.

In a home network, peer-to-peer is almost always the best choice because of its simplicity and the likelihood that you don't have very complicated resource sharing requirements. Often, you simply want to share a couple of folders (such as digital photos or music), a printer or two, and an Internet connection. None of those require a centralized server.

How do you make the choice between server-based, peer-to-peer, or a combination of the two? In general, if you have a business with more than about 10 users and need to provide secure access to shared resources, a server-based network is my recommendation. Centralizing the shared resources on a server will also result in a simplified backup strategy. Perhaps more important, this type of network provides much greater security to protect confidential and private data.

If yours is a small company with fewer than 10 users and you want to reduce your costs as much as possible, consider using a computer running Windows XP Professional as your server (but weigh the benefits of greater security against the cost for the server and operating system). If you're putting in a home network, it's likely that you won't need a centralized server of any kind, but can instead use peer-to-peer networking.

Is It Too Much For You To Tackle?

My philosophy has always been that if you can read and understand, you can do. I've built a house, rebuilt engines, built furniture, designed networks, and accomplished lots of other fairly complicated tasks with little more than a can-do attitude and a good book on the subject—but I wouldn't tackle brain surgery unless I absolutely had to.

Is there anything too difficult for the average lay person to accomplish in setting up a network? Absolutely not! With the advice and directions you'll find in this book, you'll be able to tackle any part of the network design and implementation. But like any task, there might be pieces of the puzzle that you will want to leave to others because of the time involved. For example, I just finished a large addition to a house, and contracted out the foundation work. I could have laid the block, but I wanted to make sure it was done right. Plus, what took a mason two days to accomplish would have taken me two weeks—and the results would not have been nearly as good.

Even if you've never run a cable or looked inside a computer, however, there is absolutely nothing involved in setting up a network that you can't accomplish with a little bit of study and a little bit of time. After all, it's not brain surgery or rocket science!

It's Not Just For Computers!

As you begin to plan your network, keep in mind that networks are not just for computers and printers anymore. Personal Digital Assistants (PDAs), cell phones, and other devices—whether wired or wireless—could be an important part of your day and therefore good candidates for tying into your network.

These types of traditional devices aren't the only ones you might want to tie into your networks. Streaming audio is a good example. There are hundreds of online radio stations around the globe and devices that enable you to stream that music to your stereo over a wireless connection. You might have or be thinking about buying a Media Center PC, which integrates audio, video, and TV through a combination of computer and TV. You'll want that PC on the Internet to download music, TV schedules, and other media. For an example of some new multimedia network gadgets, check out www.linksys.com and www.dlink.com, two manufacturers of networking devices.

Then, look beyond entertainment and computing to your refrigerator. Yes, you read correctly—refrigerator. Some of today's major appliances (and certainly almost all of tomorrow's) include the capability to connect to a network to allow remote troubleshooting, reprogramming, and even limited repair across the Internet. Powerline networking and low-range wireless technologies will be the most common means to connect these devices to the network. So, don't run an Ethernet cable to your refrigerator and oven just yet, but if you want a totally connected home, keep the future in mind as you build your network.

Finally, if you're planning to build or buy a new home in the near future, think networking going in. More and more new homes today are not only wired for a data network in every room, but provide cabling for surveillance systems, distributed audio, and lots more. Check out www.broadbandutopia.com for more information on structured wiring and building a connected home.

Summary

Many reasons exist for adding a network, and most common is the capability a network provides for sharing files and printers. Sharing can be almost as important in a home network as in a small business, providing convenience, reducing duplication, and simply making your computers more useful. All of that translates into more productivity and a better user experience.

Several options exist for networking, both in how you structure the network and in whether you use wired, wireless, or a combination of the two. Other technologies such as Power-over-Ethernet and powerline networking also extend networking capability beyond traditional boundaries.

Putting together a network is by no means beyond the average computer user. Armed with an understanding of key terms and techniques, you can successfully plan and implement a secure and functional network to suit all of your needs.

Chapter 2

Choosing the Right Network Infrastructure

There is no magic formula to choosing a network infrastructure for your home or small office. However, there are several points you need to consider. This chapter explores the impact the Internet will have on your network solution and give you some ideas for sharing an Internet connection among multiple users. This chapter also explores network speed, both in terms of the local area network and the Internet.

It's a good bet that sooner or later you'll want to provide wireless connectivity for your network, and this chapter explores wireless options and how they fare against wired options for speed and security. It also covers powerline networking and Power-Over-Ethernet to help you factor those two technologies into the picture. The chapter finishes with a look a network topology options, or the physical way in which the network is structured.

The Internet Factor

Not too many years ago, most companies looking to add a network wanted file and printer sharing and little else. Today, providing distributed Internet access has become almost as important as resource sharing (sometimes more important). Many home users are looking to provide a shared Internet connection for their computers, and file and printer sharing is secondary. So, one of your first considerations when planning a small network should be whether the Internet factors into the picture.

Types of Broadband Connections

Whether you are setting up a home network or a business network, it's likely that sooner rather than later you'll be tying your network to the Internet through a broadband connection. Here's a brief overview of the four most common types of broadband Internet connections:

▶ **Asymmetric Digital Subscriber Line (ADSL)** — ADSL uses a standard phone line to connect your network to the Internet. The phone line can piggyback on an existing voice line, meaning your telephone and Internet share the same physical phone line. However, the presence of DSL has no effect on voice calls and vice-versa. You can still use the phone while using the Internet, although the provider must install a filter to essentially separate the phone and Internet to prevent interference for your voice calls. The filter can be installed upstream of all phones, or you can use a small filter at each phone jack. A special DSL modem separates the Internet traffic and serves as the connection point between the network and the Internet.

> *Note:*
>
> ADSL is just one implementation of DSL. Others, including SDLS, HDSL, and VDSL, are used for networking scenarios. However, ADSL is currently the most common implementation for providing broadband Internet connectivity. ADSL supports downstream speeds from 64Kbps to 28Mbps and upstream speeds in the range of 64Kbps to 512Kbps dependent upon the distance from the customer's premises to the provider's central office. The closer you are, the higher the possible performance.

▶ **Cable** — This broadband option piggybacks on your Cable TV connection. A special cable modem separates the TV and Internet signals and provides the connection between your network and the Internet. It isn't uncommon to see 3Mbps downstream speeds in areas where DSL offerings max out at 1.544Mbps. Cost is comparable with DSL. No additional phone line is required.

▶ **T1 or Fractional T1** — A T1 is a dedicated phone line consisting of 24 channels, each of which supports 64Kbps. A full T1 therefore supports 1.544Mbps. Most providers will offer fractional T1 connections, which means that you use only a certain number of channels and pay for the bandwidth those channels provide. T1 lines are sometimes referred to as DS1 lines.

▶ **Frame Relay** — This is actually a packet-switching protocol for connecting devices on a wide area network (WAN). Frame relay works over a T1 or fractional T1 line. In the United States, frame relay supports connections from 56Kbps to 1.544Mbps (although frame relay can also support up to T3, or 45Mbps). It is most commonly used to seamlessly connect remote office locations to a corporate headquarters.

▶ **Wireless** — Although not as common as the previous four options, wireless broadband is available in some markets, typically where the other options are not available. A wireless transceiver and antenna serve as the connection point to the provider's network. In general, you must install an external antenna for this type of broadband. Wireless networks are subject to much more interference from environmental elements than the other options, and like cable, must compete with other customers' signals.

Each of these offers high speed and is an acceptable option. For home networks, I recommend either DSL or cable. Both provide comparable performance, although in my experience DSL is less susceptible to saturation, in which a large number of customers on the same circuit can degrade the circuit's performance. However, the performance of each is entirely dependent on how the provider provisions and allocates the circuit, so DSL is not necessarily any better a solution than cable.

Make your decision based on availability and price, but keep in mind that the number of other subscribers on your cable connection could impact your Internet connection's performance. Check with the providers in your area to determine what type of performance you can expect with each offering.

Note:

Like DSL, cable is generally configured with different downstream/upstream speeds. For example, a cable package that offers 3Mbps downstream might offer a max of 256Mbps upstream. So, downloads will be much faster than uploads, but that isn't an issue for most people.

Both DSL and cable are certainly workable solutions for small businesses, and the cost for each is comparable. Most providers offer different packages and prices for varying levels of performance. If you need to ensure reliability and a quick response to service issues, choose a T1 line rather than DSL or cable. Frame relay is also a reliable solution, but dependent upon the provider's network saturation levels. A straight T1 line will generally provide better throughput than frame relay.

If you intend to host your own Web services, consider the impact of that hosting on your Internet connection. A server that sees relatively little traffic can exist quite nicely on a DSL or cable connection. Keep in mind that your upstream speed will be slower than your downstream speed—remote users will experience your upstream speeds for data they pull from your servers.

Tech Tip:

Run, don't walk away from hosting your own Web site if you need to provide reliable access to it, particularly for e-commerce applications. Outsource your hosting to a reliable hosting company that can manage your server, perform backups, and has a 24x7 staff on hand to deal with outages or other problems. The minimal cost of outsourcing your Web hosting to a company that specializes in it is definitely worthwhile.

Sharing a Home Internet Connection

There are two common Internet access options available today: dial-up and broadband.

With a dial-up connection, your computer connects to an Internet Service Provider's (ISP) network through a modem connected to a phone line on an as-needed basis. Typical dial-up connections offer from 28Kbps to 56Kbps connection speeds. If you do relatively little surfing and mainly use your Internet account for e-mail, a dial-up connection isn't a bad option. Granted, dial-up connections are generally less reliable and certainly slower than broadband connections, but they can still be an inexpensive and viable option.

You can certainly share a dial-up connection to the Internet—you don't need a modem in each computer. Windows 98 and later include a feature called Internet Connection Sharing (ICS) that enables one computer to serve as the connection point, while other computers access the Internet through its modem across the network. In effect, the computer hosting the modem acts as an Internet gateway for the network. When a computer on the network submits a network request for a resource on the Internet (such as when a user opens a Web browser), the computer hosting the modem dials the Internet and routes the traffic between the other computer and the Internet. Figure 2.1 shows such a network.

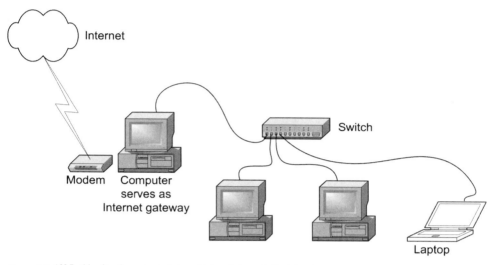

Figure 2.1: ICS Enables One Computer to Act as a Dial-up Gateway to the Internet.

A broadband connection offers and always-on connection to the Internet so there is no lag time between when you open the browser and when the page starts to load—there is no dialing time. Perhaps more important, a broadband connection provides significantly higher speed than a dial-up. While the maximum dial-up speed is slightly less than 56Kbps, typical broadband connections for SOHO users range from 256Kbps to 1.5Mbps. So, the slowest broadband connection is at least four times as fast as the fastest dial-up—in most cases, they are usually faster. More important, the perceived throughput is often faster with a broadband connection than with a dial-up.

You can share a broadband Internet connection in one of two ways. The first is to use ICS in Windows to share the connection, much like you would when sharing a dial-up connection. Figure 2.2 shows this type of Internet sharing scenario.

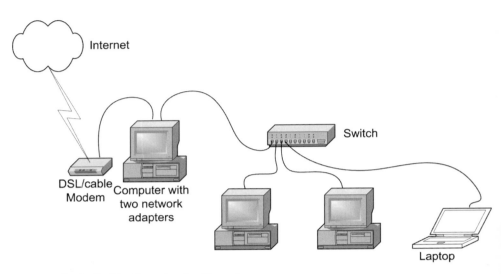

Figure 2.2: You Can Use ICS to Share a Broadband Connection.

A better approach to sharing a broadband connection is to use a broadband router, which sits between your broadband connection (cable or DSL modem) and your network (see Figure 2.3). In this scenario, the broadband router, rather than a computer, serves as the gateway for the network.

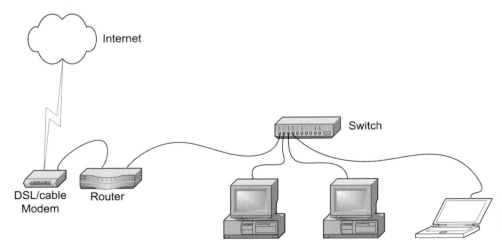

Figure 2.3: A Broadband Router Serves as an Internet Gateway.

This latter approach offers a couple of advantages:

▶ **Security** — Most broadband routers include at least a basic firewall. The firewall blocks unwanted traffic from connecting to systems inside your network. This helps reduce the threat of worms and other superfluous network traffic from reaching your computers and potentially causing disruptions or loss of data.

▶ **Simplicity and reliability** — It isn't difficult to configure ICS, but neither is it particularly difficult to configure a broadband router. So, configuration is roughly the same for each approach. However, when you move the routing and other gateway functions from a computer to a dedicated broadband router, you eliminate the need for the gateway computer to be on all the time. You can rearrange computers, reinstall operating systems, and make changes to a computer without worrying whether it will affect the ability of other users to access the Internet.

▶ **Content Filtering** — Some broadband routers, in addition to providing firewall services, also provide content filtering services. A content filter blocks Web sites based on a variety of criteria, such as adult content, weapons, language, and so on. Generally, you must subscribe to a filter list provider to use the content filter feature.

Here are the decisions you need to make at this point:

▶ Will you continue to use a dial-up connection or switch to broadband?

▶ Will you be sharing the Internet connection through ICS?

▶ If you have a broadband connection, will you use ICS or a broadband router?

▶ Does the router have a firewall in place or will you need a separate firewall (or firewall software at each computer)?

▶ Do you want to add content filtering to your Internet connection for all computers?

Connecting Your Office to the Internet

Many of the issues related to the Internet that apply to a home network also apply to an office network. However, it's much less likely that you will be considering using a dial-up connection. The relatively low cost for a broadband connection is easily justified by most companies, particularly where multiple users need concurrent access to the Internet. So, I'll assume you'll be connecting to the Internet with a broadband connection.

Most likely, you will use a DSL connection because of the lesser cost compared to a T1 or fractional T1 line. If you choose DSL, configuration will be somewhat easier than for a T1 because most DSL routers are geared toward nontechnical users and offer easy configuration through a Web page. By contrast, a T1 requires a more sophisticated router with more sophisticated setup issues. In short, it's likely you'll be able to set up your own DSL router configuration, but you'll likely need assistance from your provider to configure your router for a T1 or fractional T1 connection. In many cases, the provider programs the router for you as part of the circuit installation and associated cost.

The router that you install will enable users on the network to share the Internet connection. However, there are other issues to consider as well, including how the computers will receive their IP addresses and other TCP/IP configuration data. For details, see Chapter 5, which also covers how to configure broadband connections.

Security

Whether yours is a home or a business network, security should be a major consideration. In all cases, any network that is connected to the Internet should be protected by a firewall at the gateway. Why not simply install firewall software at each computer? By using a firewall at the gateway, you centralize and simplify firewall administration. You also eliminate the possibility that a user will turn off his or her firewall software or even uninstall it. There is nothing at all wrong with using local firewalls in addition to a gateway firewall to supplement and enhance network security. See Chapter 6 for a complete discussion of firewalls.

In addition to a firewall, you should also plan to implement other security measures, depending on the network's structure and how you use it. A security policy outlining what is and isn't permitted on work computers is a good start to securing systems. Educating users about potential security risks in a business network will greatly reduce the chance of downtime due to virus infections and malware. Consider the following points:

▶ **Physical security** — Physical access to routers, firewalls, and other Internet connection devices should be restricted. Ideally, these should be located in a locked server room. Servers, if any, should be kept under lock, as well. Only those responsible for administering the equipment should have physical access to it.

▶ **Server security** — In addition to physically securing servers, you should implement policies with your administrator(s) to further secure the servers. For example, servers should never be left in a logged-on state. Strong passwords should be used for all administrative accounts. Administrator account status should be given only to those users who need to manage the server as a whole; lesser levels of access can be allocated to individuals who need to manage only certain aspects of the server or its applications.

Note:

See Chapter 8 for details on setting up and using user and administrator accounts.

▶ **Workstation security** — Workstations should be secured with accounts and strong passwords. Users should be required to change passwords on a regular basis (this recommendation applies more to a business network than a home network). Floppy disk drives and other removable recordable media (not including CD drives) should be disabled or removed unless users specifically need them to accomplish their jobs. These devices are a potential source of virus infection and weak point for securing confidential or proprietary data.

Tech Tip:

Consider using Information Rights Management with Microsoft Office applications including Outlook to secure proprietary data. See www.microsoft.com/technet/ prodtechnol/office/office2003/operate/of03irm.mspx **or** *Microsoft Office Outlook 2003 Inside Out* from Microsoft Press (2003) for details on using IRM.

▶ **Wireless security** — Wireless networks are inherently less secure than wired networks. If you implement a wireless solution, make sure you take all possible steps to prevent unauthorized use of the network and to prevent data from being hijacked. See Chapter 9 for specifics.

How Speed Figures Into the Picture

If you're going to the trouble and expense of installing a network, you probably want the fastest one possible. After all, you won't get great Internet performance without a fast network, right? Well, that's actually a wrong assumption in most cases. You're about to read some number comparisons, but don't let your eyes glaze over—I'll offer a lay summary shortly.

The typical maximum broadband connection speed in a SOHO network is from 1.544Mbps to 3Mbps. By contrast, even the slowest of today's Ethernet networks operates at 10Mbps, nearly 6.5 times faster than the Internet connection. So, even a slow network will be fine for most Internet browsing tasks, because the Internet connection will be the slow link, not the local area network (LAN).

However, LAN speed is an important consideration for local network operations such as copying files or streaming media (audio or video) from a local server. For example, if you copy or move a 1GB file (or group of files) between computers on a 10Mbps network, the theoretical transfer time would be about 14 minutes:

8,589,934,592 bits / 10,000,000 bits/second = 859 seconds

By contrast, the same amount of data transferred over a 100Mbps LAN would take (theoretically), just over 8 seconds. On a 1Gbps LAN, the transfer would theoretically be less than a second. Realistically, speeds are not that high due to several factors, but you can see that a faster network can have a huge impact on network performance.

Tech Tip:

Would you really transfer that much data around? You might be moving your collection of digital photos, a set of downloaded files, large application files such as drawings, and so on. Even if you do this infrequently, the cost to have a faster network isn't exorbitant and generally well worth the additional cost.

Today, the general standard for a basic network is 100Mbps. Most network adapters, hubs, and switches sold today will support 10/100Mbps, meaning that they handle both 10Mbps and 100Mbps devices on the same network.

1Gbps networks offer roughly 10 times the theoretical top-end speed of a 100Mbps network, making them a great option where LAN performance is critical. 10Gbps networks are available but not commonplace. The newness of the technology places the cost outside the reach of most businesses.

So, let's put these numbers into perspective. Assume you install a DSL or cable Internet connection—a reasonable assumption for a home or small business installation. Table 2.1 shows how much faster your LAN will be than your Internet connection.

Internet	LAN	Times faster (LAN versus Internet)
256Kbps	10Mbps	40
256Kbps	100Mbps	400
256Kbps	1Gbps	4096
512Kbps	10Mbps	20
512Kbps	100Mbps	200
512Kbps	1Gbps	2048
1.544Mbps	100Mbps	65

Table 2.1: Comparison of Internet versus LAN speeds.

As Table 2.1 shows, even the slowest LAN is going to be roughly 40 times faster than the slowest typical broadband Internet connection. So, it's all about what you want to do on the local network, not how fast you want to be able to surf the Internet.

What About Cabling and Hardware Costs?

Cat5e cable, commonly used for most LAN installations, handles 100Mbps with no problem. In fact, Cat5e can handle a 1Gbps network. So, you can install Cat5e cable and be assured that you can move up to 1Gbps, either initially or down the road. If you want to be able to move beyond 1Gbps to 10Gpbs, consider installing Cat6 cable.

Note:

Though you could install fiber optic cable on your LAN, it won't increase the capacity and is generally not worth the additional cost or labor involved. If you can get 10Gbs out of a copper cable, why hassle with fiber?

The cost for hardware is not significantly higher to move from 100Mbps to 1Gbps. Network adapters, for example, are roughly the same cost. The cost difference in switches is somewhat more. I estimate that in a 10-computer network, the cost difference to go from 100Mbps to 1Gbps could easily be less than $200.

Tech Tip:

Install switches rather than hubs to provide the best LAN throughput. See Chapter 3 for details.

What's the Bottom Line?

I recommend that if you are installing a wired network, you should install at least Cat5e cable, which will support up to 1Gbps. If you are looking at 10Gbps down the road for business purposes, or are interested in such things as streaming HDTV in the future, Cat6 is the way to go. It's a little more expensive (about twice as much as I write this), but why run cable twice? If I were going to re-cable my home or install a new office network, I'd choose Cat6. If you're installing a home network and just want to connect computers without worrying about streaming TV or other media in the future, Cat5e is a great, less expensive option.

As for the network hardware, I recommend 1Gbps for both business and home networks. However, there is no real downside to choosing 10/100Mbps if you want to save some money now. You can always replace the network adapters and switches later to move up to 1Gbps (as long as you use Cat5e or better cabling). See Chapter 3 for recommendations on hardware.

Wired Versus Wireless

How does wireless fit into picture when you're trying to plan your network? There are several issues to consider.

Performance

Although wireless networks have come a long way in terms of speed, they can't match today's wired speeds. There are three common wireless options available today:

▶ **802.11a** — This standard supports up to 54Mbps and operates in the unsaturated 5GHz band. Typical range is from 25-75 feet indoors. Public hotspots are generally unavailable.

▶ **802.11b** — This standard provides for up to 11Mbps data rates and is readily available. Many public hotspots support 802.11b. It operates in the relatively saturated 2.4GHz band with cordless phones and certain other devices. Typical range is from 100-150 feet indoors.

▶ **802.11g** — This standard supports up to 54Mbps and operates in the 2.4GHz band. It is backward compatible with 802.11b at 11Mbps, and G-band public hotspots are becoming much more common. It is not compatible with 802.11a.

802.11g has seen a lot of growth and has quickly become the wireless option of choice. 802.11b is somewhat less expensive, but the relatively low cost for 802.11g access points and other hardware make 802.11g my recommended solution.

Tech Tip:

I jumped on the A/G bandwagon and purchased an access point that supports both A and G bands when it first came out. Now, I wish I had opted for a straight G device. Because of A-band's higher frequency, I can't add a range extender to my access point. Plus, the A/G device was three to four times the cost of a straight G access point. Unless you have a compelling reason to support both A and G, choose G.

What About Bluetooth?? *Bluetooth* **is a wireless networking standard that offers low-range wireless networking for low-load devices such as PDAs and headsets. Bluetooth provides a range from 10 to 100 meters depending on class. It supports up to 1MB/s transfer rate. In short, Bluetooth is not intended to connect computers. Rather, it is used to connect smaller devices with lower transfer requirements to computers, phones, and other equipment.**

Security

Both wired and wireless networks should incorporate a firewall at the Internet gateway to protect the LAN from Internet-based threats. So, let's take a look at security differences between wired and wireless networks from the LAN side.

Wireless networks are inherently less secure than wired networks. It is very difficult to snoop on a wired network without physical access to the network, unless a hacker is successful in planting a sniffer of some kind via a virus or Trojan. A *sniffer* monitors and reports on network traffic. Wireless networks are susceptible to sniffing because anyone within range of the network can potentially gain access to the network, depending on the network's security configuration.

There are many steps you can take to secure a wireless network, and Chapter 9 covers wireless security in detail. For now, understand that if you intend to implement a wireless network or a wireless segment on your wired network, you'll need to take additional configuration steps to make sure your network is secured against unauthorized access and the potential for data or bandwidth theft.

Flexibility and Convenience

A wired network requires a physical connection anywhere you want to connect a computer to the network. Wireless networks only require that wireless-enabled devices be within range of an access point. Wireless access can be a wonderful addition to the network, whether at home or work. You can use your notebook or PDA almost anywhere. For example, you could work from your deck, sofa, or conference room.

Wireless access also simplifies networking by eliminating the need to run cables. This is a big issue in buildings where it isn't practical to run cables because of the building's design or construction. As you plan your network, keep in mind that wireless could well overcome physical barriers and add considerable convenience to the network, with the tradeoff being somewhat slower overall performance. However, you might have to place multiple access points to provide full coverage for the building.

Tech Tip:

At 54Mbps, an 802.11g wireless network is about half the speed of a 100Mbps network, but that speed is fine for the vast majority of home and small business users.

Powerline Networking

Where wireless access isn't necessary and running cable isn't feasible, a good alternative is powerline networking. As explained in Chapter 1, powerline networking uses the building's electrical cabling as the network. Today, powerline networking supports up to 3Mbps transfer rates, with higher rates possible as the technology continues to mature.

If you're looking for a very easy way to implement a home network and Web browsing is your main use for the network, then powerline networking is a great option. If you need higher performance, look to wireless as an alternative to running cable.

> *Tech Tip:*
> Powerline networking is a handy method to network smart appliances without running additional cable.

Power-Over-Ethernet (PoE)

As explained in Chapter 1, Power-Over-Ethernet, or PoE, enables devices to be powered through the network cable that connects the devices to the network. For example, you might use PoE to power IP-based cameras in a surveillance system. Using PoE eliminates the need to run separate power to the remote devices.

> *Tech Tip:*
> Devices that require low voltage power and coaxial cable, such as analog surveillance cameras, can be wired using what is sometimes called *Siamese cable*. This cable contains the coaxial cable for the camera signal as well as low voltage wire to power the camera.

To implement PoE, you need to use a switch capable of providing PoE or add a midspan hub to the network to inject power into the twisted pair between the switch and the remote device. In addition, you should also install an uninterruptible power supply (UPS) to provide continued power for devices in the event of a power failure.

Do you need PoE for your network? There is probably no place in a home network for PoE unless you need to run power to a remote surveillance device. You probably have power accessible wherever you need to connect devices or can easily add power where needed.

PoE is more likely a requirement in a business network where the building's construction or the placement of the remote device precludes running additional electrical lines. If that's your situation, consider PoE as a solution. Otherwise, look to wireless solutions (such as wireless cameras) as a viable alternative. See `www.poweroverethernet.com` for more details on PoE.

Topology

When planning your network, you need to consider the *topology* you will use. There are four main topologies used in LANs:

▶ **Bus** — All devices in a bus topology are connected to a common cable called the *bus* or *backbone* (see Figure 2.4). Bus topology is relatively inexpensive to implement and works well in small LANs where the computers are located close to one another, such as in a lab setting in a single room.

▶ **Ring** — Devices are connected to one another in a closed loop, with each device connected to two others (see Figure 2.5). Ring topology is relatively expensive to implement but supports high transfer rates.

▶ **Star** — The star topology is by far the most common for today's small networks. Devices are connected by individual cables to a central hub or switch (see Figure 2.6). Star topology is easy to set up and scales well to larger networks, but the hub can become a bottleneck to performance. It's important to use switches rather than hubs for best performance.

▶ **Tree** — The tree topology combines star segments with a linear bus (see Figure 2.7).

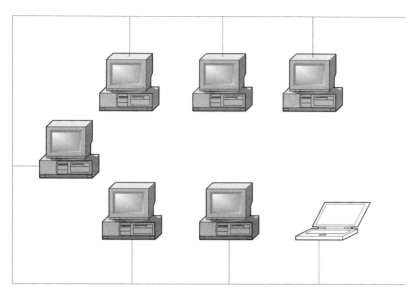

Figure 2.4: A Bus Network Topology.

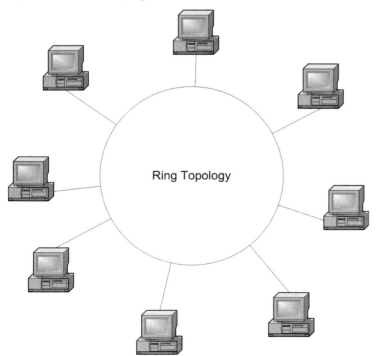

Figure 2.5: A Ring Network Topology.

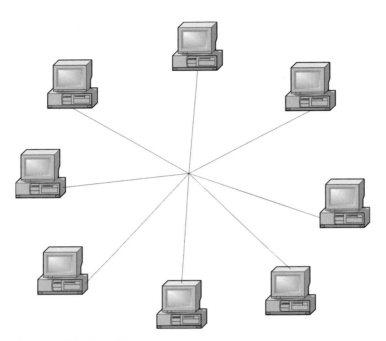

Figure 2.6: A Star Network Topology.

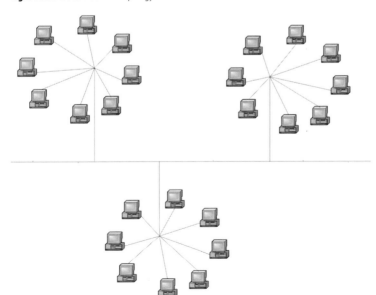

Figure 2.7: A Tree Network Topology.

Which topology is best for your network? A bus is easy to implement in a lab or office setting where all of the computers are located in the same room and around the perimeter of the room. This arrangement makes it easy to run a cable from one computer to the next. However, a bus topology usually doesn't work well when the computers are located in different offices, on multiple floors, or are not arranged in a configuration that lends itself to computer-to-computer connections.

In most cases, a star topology works best for small networks because you can run cables to multiple rooms and floors from a central wiring closet, server room, or even basement cranny where the switch or hub is located. You can scale the star topology out to multiple floors easily, as shown in Figure 2.8, by using multiple switches (and therefore multiple stars).

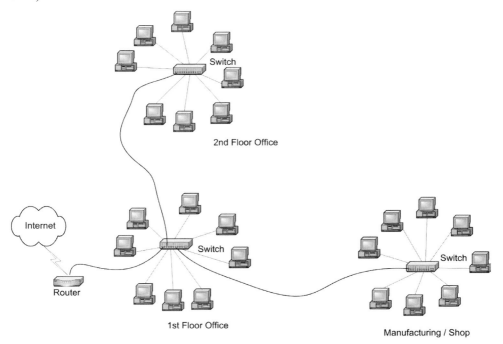

Figure 2.8: The Star Topology Can Easily Scale to Multiple Floors or Offices.

In general, ring topology and tree topologies are not applicable to SOHO networks because of the low cost and relative efficiency of bus and star topologies.

Summary

Now that you have all of this basic network background information, how do you put it together to come up with your own network plan? Easy! Start by drawing a diagram, and then determine how you will use the network:

▶ Sketch your home or office area and identify the points where you want computers or other networked devices to be located. Pick a central location for the hub or switch (see Chapter 4 for more details).

▶ Decide if wireless access will be useful. If so, explore your security requirements in detail (see Chapter 9).

▶ Determine if any of the devices will require PoE for power.

▶ Decide how fast a network you really need, based on how you use the network now and plan to use it in the future. Choose between wired and wireless (or implement a mixed solution) accordingly.

With the overall network sketched out, you're ready to start choosing the individual networking components. Chapter 3 will help you choose network cards, switches, and network infrastructure components such as cable and patch panels.

Chapter 3

Choosing Networking Components

The heart of every network is the physical infrastructure that makes it work. Choosing the right networking components can mean the difference between a reliable network and one that causes you nothing but grief—both in setting it up and using it.

This chapter offers advice on choosing your networking hardware, including network adapters, cabling and other infrastructure items, the gateway equipment to connect your network to the Internet, and wireless components. Before you rush out to buy a load of gadgets, make sure you check out this chapter!

Cabling, Hubs, and Switches

While you might think that the network adapter for your computers is the place to start, those adapters will be useless without the network infrastructure in place. So, that's where we'll start—with your network cabling.

Cabling Guidelines

Chapter 2 recommended Cat5e as a minimum for a wired network. If you want to be able to move up the bandwidth to 10Gbps and higher, and are willing to pay the additional price, Cat6 is the way to go. But choosing between Cat5e and Cat6 is just the first step. You also need to know what type of cable to buy.

The prevalent type of cable used for networking in SOHO applications is *unshielded twisted pair*, or UTP. A UTP network cable comprises four pairs of conductors, with each pair twisted together to reduce crosstalk (interference) between pairs. The cable itself is covered with a sheathing material—typically polyvinyl chloride (PVC) in less expensive cables.

When PVC burns, it emits toxic fumes. One burning cable probably won't kill you, but several might, particularly if you are a firefighter wading into a building full of network cables.

In most locales, building codes require the use of *plenum* cables in any air-handling spaces such as those above suspended ceilings or under a raised floor. The plenum cable uses a different type of jacket with safer fire characteristics. Plenum cable is more expensive than non-plenum cable, so use the plenum cable only where it's required according to your local and state building codes. Check your codes to determine what type of cable to get.

You can find Cat5e cabling at many home improvement retailers such as Home Depot and Lowes, and at other general retailers. There are many online sources for cable, including www.cablestogo.com, www.computercablestore.com, www.lanshack.com, and www.cables4sure.com, just to name a few. You're also certain to find a computer store near you that sells cable and other networking products.

What's the Difference Between a Hub and a Switch?

When you know what type of cable you need, turn your attention to the distribution point—the hub or switch.

A *hub* serves as a connection point between computers (and other devices) and the network (See Figure 3.1). The hub contains multiple ports, with each port connecting to a device, or in a more complex network, to another hub.

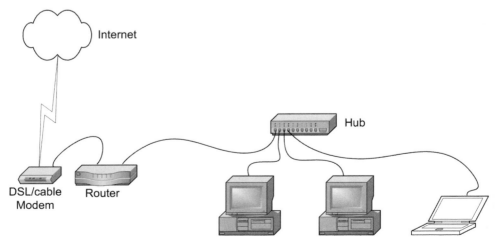

Figure 3.1: Hubs—Connection Points for Network Devices.

When a packet of data arrives at one port, the hub copies the packet to all other ports on the hub, essentially broadcasting the packet to all ports and therefore all devices. A *passive hub* does nothing other than forward packets to all ports. A *managed hub* (also called an *intelligent hub*) enables an administrator to monitor the traffic through the hub and configure certain properties for the hub's ports.

A *switching hub* (or more simply, a *switch*) like the one shown in Figure 3.2 reads the destination address for each packet and forwards the packet only to the applicable port(s). For example, when you browse the Internet, all of the data packets coming from the Web site would be broadcast to all computers on a passive hub, while on a switch the packets would be directed only to your computer. What's the difference? In short, switching hubs give better performance than passive hubs because they eliminate packet collisions.

Figure 3.2: A Typical Switch.

Only one packet can travel on a cable at any one time. If two packets are sent on a cable at the same time, a *collision* occurs. The packets must then be retransmitted, ultimately slowing down network performance. Using a switch therefore reduces network traffic and collisions because the switch sends the packet only to the destination device.

Note:

The switch automatically learns which addresses are associated with specific ports. You don't need to configure the switch in any way.

Not too many years ago, hubs were much cheaper than switches. Today, the price is very similar. For that reason, I always recommend using switches rather than hubs.

There are lots of sources for hubs and switches. Even some general retailers like Wal-Mart sell them. Your local computer store is certain to have them, as are computer-related retailers like Circuit City, Best Buy, CompUSA, and others. The online sources are also numerous.

There are also several brands of hubs and switches. LinkSys (www.linksys.com), D-Link (www.dlink.com), and Belkin (www.belkin.com) are some of the more popular companies that offer a range of products geared toward the SOHO market. In general, you'll find comparable performance from most of the manufacturers, so you can be comfortable shopping by price and availability.

Racks, Patch Panels, and Connectors

The hub or switch serves to connect one end of each network cable to the network, but what about the other end of the cable? Usually, the other end ultimately connects to a device such as a computer, network print server, router—or in larger networks—other switches. Figure 3.3 shows a typical small network.

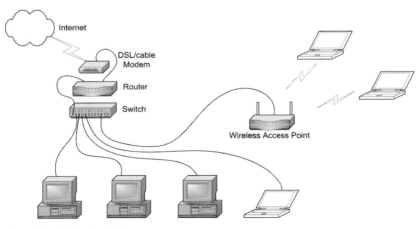

Figure 3.3: A Typical Small Network.

One way to connect a network cable to a device is to simply crimp a connector to the end of the cable and plug it into the device. The connector for a standard UTP network connection is called an RJ45 connector. Figure 3.4 shows an RJ45 connector.

Figure 3.4: An RJ45 Connector.

You can certainly buy loose RJ45 connectors and a crimping tool, then crimp the connector on the end of the cable. But should you? In a word, no.

Making crimped connections not only requires a crimping tool, but takes some practice to accomplish successfully and with any reasonable speed. Unfortunately, not every connection works, because of misaligned conductors or other problems. Also, the cable must be cut, stripped, and another connector crimped on.

What's the solution? Use a patch panel and punched connections!

Patch Panels for Convenience and Easy Setup

A *patch panel* for a UTP network cable contains several RJ45 connectors on the front and connection posts on the back (see Figure 3.5). To use a patch panel, you connect the individual conductors for a cable to the back of the panel with a special tool called a *punch-down tool*. The tool presses the wire into a set of posts that hold the wire in place and serve as the connection for the wire to a pin in one of the jacks on the front of the panel. Each jack has its own set of eight connectors on the back of the panel—connecting a cable is a matter of punching each of the eight color-coded wires to their respective color-coded posts. Too easy!

Figure 3.5: A Patch Panel.

Racks

The patch panel is typically located in a wiring closet or other central location with the switch, router, and firewall. The patch panel doesn't simply sit on a shelf, although it can. Instead, it is usually screwed to a rack or enclosure (cabinet).Racks can be wall-mounted or floor-mounted. The standard rack width is 19 inches, and hardware such as patch panels and other rack-mounted devices are designed to fit these standard racks.

In addition to holding the patch panel(s), the rack can also be used to mount devices such as switches, routers, firewalls, and power supplies. Some manufacturers offer their products in desktop or rack-mount versions. For equipment that doesn't include tabs for mounting in a rack, purchase one or more shelf units for the rack and place the equipment on a shelf.

The type of rack you choose depends on the number of devices that will mount on the rack. For mounting one or more servers with monitor and keyboard, an uninterruptible power supply (UPS), and other networking devices, a floor-mounted rack makes the most sense. For small networks that only include a router/firewall, a switch, and a patch panel, a wall-mounted rack is a great solution. In those situations where physical security of the equipment is a concern, choose a lockable cabinet.

When you're choosing your rack or enclosure, keep in mind the many accessories that are available for them, including:

► **Cable management panel** — These panels include D-rings that help organize cables and keep them from draping all over the front of the rack. Use these in combination with cable straps (either plastic or Velcro™) to neatly organize cables.

▶ **Cable strain relief bar** — These bars mount in the back of the rack and provide a place to attach cables so they don't hang from and place a strain on patch panel connections or networking devices.

▶ **Keyboard drawer** — These rack-mounted drawers are designed to hold a keyboard for rack-mounted servers.

▶ **Equipment shelf** — An equipment shelf holds devices such as switches and routers that don't include mounting tabs for mounting to the rack itself. Choose vented shelves in situations where the shelf is located above a server or other device that needs venting, or when heat-producing equipment will be placed on the shelf and the equipment vents through the bottom.

▶ **Center-weighted equipment shelf** — Choose a center-weighted equipment shelf for heavier items such as a monitor or a UPS.

▶ **KVM switches** — KVM stands for Keyboard, Video, and Mouse. Use these devices to connect a single keyboard, mouse, and monitor to more than one rack-mounted server.

▶ **Rack-mounted equipment** — Many networking and server-related devices are available in rack-mounted versions. These include switches, routers, firewalls, UPS, servers, and even monitors. Also consider a rack-mounted UPS, cooling fan units, and other support equipment if you're setting up one or more rack-mounted servers with your networking hardware. Install heavy equipment at the bottom of the rack for stability.

Tech Tip:
Include a UPS for the switch, router, firewall, and other equipment to avoid reboots and downtime when the power fails.

Racks are sized by *units* (called *spaces* by some manufacturers), and each device takes up a certain number of units. For example, a cable management panel might take up two rack units. A blade server might take up one unit. Decide what you will place on your rack now and in the near future and plan accordingly. Allow space for the devices you'll install right away, and allow room for expansion in the future.

Patch Cables and Receptacles

The network distribution cables in a clean network installation connect to a patch panel, but what connects to the patch panel? What connects the computer or print server to the distribution cable at the other end? The best option is to use a *patch cable*.

A patch cable is a short cable (typically one to two meters) with network connectors on each end. One end of the patch cable connects to the patch panel and the other connects to the device (such as a switch).

Tech Tip:

As with distribution cables, don't use self-crimped cables if possible. I recommend you use pre-manufactured patch cables to eliminate the effort and potential error in making your own.

At the other end of the cable—where the computer or print server must be connected to the network—use a manufactured receptacle rather than crimping a connector on the cable end. Figure 3.6 shows a typical modular receptacle. These fit in a recessed box (use the same box as you would for an electrical receptacle) or an externally-mounted box. Many modular receptacle blanks (faceplate with mounting slots) accommodate multiple connectors. For example, you might wire a network connection, phone connection, and cable TV connection in a single box. Or perhaps you need multiple network connections at a specific location. Whatever the case, choose the blanks and modules you need to accommodate the devices at each location.

Figure 3.6: A Typical Modular Receptacle.

Tech Tip:

You'll find blanks, modules, patch cables, and other wiring items at home improvement retailers like Home Depot, Lowes, and others, as well as at many computer retailers.

Note:

If you will be running cables externally on a wall, consider using *raceway* to cover the cable. Raceway is a manufactured surface-mount conduit to cover cables. You'll find plastic raceway at most of the same stores and online sites where you buy your blanks and modules.

The Gateway (Routers and Firewalls)

At the connection between the Internet and your network sits your router and firewall. In some cases, the router and firewall are the same device. This section of the chapter will help you choose the router and firewall devices that are right for your network.

Choosing a Router

The type of router you choose is almost completely dependent on the type of connection between your network and the Internet. For example, you'll need a DSL/cable router (see Figure 3.7) if your network connects to the Internet by a DSL or cable connection.

Figure 3.7: A Typical DSL/Cable Router for a Small Network.

Routers for T1-based connections will generally be more expensive than a DSL/cable router. In many cases, your ISP will offer recommendations for what router to use and in some cases will install the router for you. In any case, you need to make sure the router you choose will support the options required by your provider. For example, a frame-relay connection (frame relay is a packet-switching protocol) requires a router that supports frame-relay. Check with your ISP to determine what type of router your connection requires.

Cisco (www.cisco.com) is one of the most popular brands of router in use today, but is certainly not the only brand. Others to consider are Netgear (www.netgear.com, owned by Cisco), Nortel (www.nortel.com), SMC (www.smc.com), LinkSys (www.linksys.com), and D-Link (www.dlink.com). These latter two manufacturers offer several products for the SOHO market.

VPN Support and Routing Protocols

When choosing a router, also take into account the requirements for your network and the way you will use the network. For example, if you need to support incoming virtual private network (VPN) connections, choose a router that offers VPN capability. If you are using a T1 or fractional T1 connection, you must also consider routing protocols. Check with your ISP to determine if your router must support Router Interface Protocol (RIP), which enables routers to share routing information. The alternative to using a routing protocol is to create static routes in the router. See Chapter 5 for more discussion of routing and router configuration.

Network Address Translation and Port Forwarding

Most often, an ISP will offer a small number of public IP addresses for a customer. Home users generally receive a single public IP address. Small business users often receive from one to five public addresses. Most ISPs offer different packages with varying numbers of public addresses. Whether you need more than one depends on the services your network will offer to the outside world and how you structure your network.

Routers provide *network address translation* (NAT) to enable the LAN to use private IP addresses. The router keeps track of the packets going to and from the LAN and makes sure the packets get to the right destination.

Note:

Private IP addresses help hide your network from the outside world and offer much greater flexibility of network configuration. Plus, you'll have to pay for additional public IP addresses if you want more than one or two.

Most routers support NAT, enabling the router to host one public IP address and route traffic to and from multiple devices on the LAN. Essentially all DSL/cable routers provide this type of NAT. When one of the computers on your LAN browses the Internet, the remote server doesn't know the private IP address of the computer; instead, it sees the public IP address of the router.

Some routers also support one-to-one NAT, in which one public address is explicitly associated with one private address. Traffic that comes in to the specified public address is directed by the router to the private address you have configured in the router for that public address. For example, you might configure one public/private pair to associate your Web server with a particular LAN address and another pair for your mail server.

Tech Tip:

In some situations, you might associate one public IP with a range of private addresses. A server farm comprising multiple servers all hosting the same type of service (such as a Web server farm) is a candidate for this type of NAT arrangement. However, it's also not likely in most small business networks.

Whether or not your router must support one-to-one NAT depends on whether you need to associate multiple public IP addresses with multiple private IP addresses on the LAN. For example, if your network will contain multiple servers for public services (Web, mail, FTP, etc.), and those servers need separate public IP addresses, your router will need to support one-to-one NAT for the number of public/private address pairs you will use. But one-to-one NAT isn't always necessary.

If you only need to expose one public IP address, you can use *port forwarding* rather than one-to-one NAT. With port forwarding, the router listens for packets destined for a specific port. When that traffic arrives, the router forwards the traffic to the internal IP address on the LAN that you have designated for that port. Figure 3.8 shows the port-forwarding configuration page for a Netgear firewall.

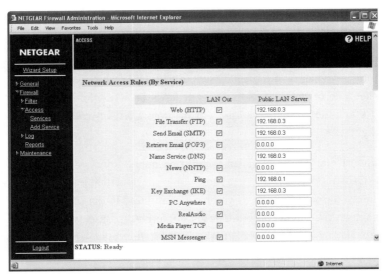

Figure 3.8: Port-Forwarding Directs Traffic to Various Computers.

Each unique service uses its own port. For example, HTTP (Web) uses port 80, FTP uses port 21, POP3 uses port 110, and SMTP uses port 25. So, assume you need to host a Web server and a mail server. The Web server requires all incoming port 80 traffic be routed to it, and the mail server requires all incoming traffic for ports 25 and 110 to be routed to it. Both servers can be represented by a single public IP address. The router simply uses port forwarding to route the traffic based on port, rather than address. Figure 3.9 illustrates the concept of using port forwarding rather than NAT when only one public IP address is required.

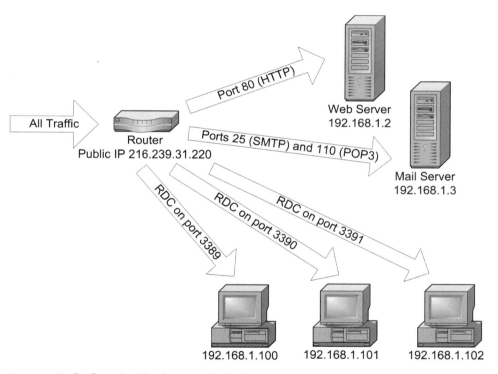

Figure 3.9: Use Port Forwarding When Only One Public IP Address Is Required.

Which is right for you: one-to-one NAT or port forwarding? In general, you only need one-to-one NAT when you must associate more than one public IP address with multiple private addresses on the LAN. Typically, the only time you need to use multiple public IP addresses is when you host the same service (and therefore use the same port) on multiple internal computers.

Tech Tip:

You don't need one-to-one NAT to support multiple incoming connections for Windows' Remote Desktop Connection (RDC). You can configure each user's computer for a unique RDC port, and then use port forwarding to forward the specified port to the appropriate computer. See Microsoft Knowledge Base documents **306759** (http://support.microsoft.com/default. aspx?scid=kb;en-us;306759) **and 304304** (http://support.microsoft.com/default. aspx?scid=kb;en-us;304304) to learn more.

See Chapter 5 for more on NAT and port forwarding.

Choosing a Firewall

No network with a connection to the Internet is complete (or safe) without a firewall. The firewall controls the types of traffic that reach the LAN (and what traffic can leave the LAN for the Internet). The firewall helps isolate the LAN from the Internet and protect the computers on the network from direct attack. The firewall also helps prevent denial-of-service (DoS) and other types of network attacks against the network and the computers that reside on the network.

Some routers incorporate a firewall. For example, many DSL/cable routers include a built-in firewall that offers basic functionality. These rudimentary firewalls enable you to block unneeded ports and help protect the network against common types of port-based attacks. In many cases, these firewalls are sufficient for home and small office users. However, a more full-featured firewall does have its advantages, as explained in the following sections.

Routing

A firewall can also function as a router, so you can often install a single device rather than a combination router/firewall. When you're shopping for network hardware, keep in mind that you don't necessarily need a firewall and a router—the firewall can probably do it all, particularly for DSL/cable broadband connections, while providing better network security.

Advanced Traffic Handling

While more often used in larger organizations, features that provide advanced traffic handling can have a place in smaller networks. The ability to create firewall rules that allow or disallow certain types of traffic for specific computers or groups of computers can be very useful. For example, you might need to allow incoming traffic on a specific port to a small number of computers but block it for others. Or perhaps you want to allow outgoing telnet access for a selected number of users but block it for others. Whatever the situation, the ability to define rules that control traffic in this way requires more than the typical firewall built into DSL/cable routers or lower-end stand-alone firewalls.

If you want to be able to exert a fine level of control over network traffic, investigate the rules capability offered by the firewall. Several manufacturers offer firewalls suitable (and priced) for the SOHO market that offer such capability. In particular, check out SonicWALL (www.sonicwall.com), Checkpoint (www.checkpoint.com), Netgear (www.netgear.com), and Symantec (www.symantec.com).

VPN Support

You have two common options for supporting VPN connections into your network—allow the firewall to handle VPN, or install a VPN server such as Windows Server 2003's Routing and Remote Access Services (RRAS). Using a VPN-capable firewall simplifies network configuration and management because you need only configure and manage one device. If VPN is requirement of your network, consider a VPN-capable firewall.

Content Filtering

Many firewalls support content filtering, in which the firewall blocks Web content based on URLs and categories. In a typical scenario, you purchase a six-month or one-year content filter subscription that provides updates to the URL list for that period. The firewall actively monitors Web requests and blocks attempts to access sites that you have blocked, either implicitly by content category or explicitly by URL.

Antivirus

Many mid- to high-end firewalls add the capability to scan for and block viruses and code that propagates worms. This capability can be an important additional step to protect your network from these threats. Whatever firewall solution you choose, however, don't rely on a single point for antivirus protection. I recommend antivirus protection at each computer, even with a gateway antivirus solution in place.

Network Interface Cards

Without a network interface card (NIC) of some kind, your computers won't connect to the network, so they are an important part of your network planning. But why have I left these for relatively late in the hardware discussion?

NICs are important in a general way to the users, but they are relatively unimportant from an overall network standpoint. The infrastructure, firewall, and router are most important from an administrative perspective. It's important to choose a good NIC, but it's even more important that you have a secure, well-performing network in place beforehand.

Choosing NICs

NICs aren't a dime a dozen, but like other computer hardware, they have certainly dropped in price. Many newer computers have the NIC integrated on the motherboard, eliminating the need in most cases for a separate NIC. For that reason, your first step should be to inventory the computers in your home or office and determine how many, if any, will require a NIC.

When you've determined how many NICs you need for your network, keep these points in mind when shopping for them:

▶ **Speed** — The NICs you choose must meet the speed requirements of the LAN. If you are implementing a 100Mbps network, for example, a 10Mbps card won't suffice—you need a 10/100Mbps NIC. Likewise, a 1Gbps network requires a 1Gbps NIC. Choose NICs that support the network's maximum speed.

▶ **Compatibility** — Generally speaking, you can choose NICs from almost any manufacturer and build a functioning network. However, my experience has been that consistency and simplicity can help you avoid performance and configuration problems. Identify a NIC from a well-known vendor that has drivers for your operating system(s) and standardize on one brand and model, at least initially. Doing so will make simplify configuration and driver updates/management.

▶ **Driver availability** — Verify that the vendor for the card you choose offers a driver specifically for the operating system(s) in use on your network. Choosing a known vendor with a proven track record will help ensure that updated drivers will continue to be available.

▶ **Network boot / RIS** — If you intend to implement diskless workstations in your network, those workstations must contain network adapters that enable the computer to boot across the network. If you are considering using Remote Installation Services (RIS), a service included with Windows 2000 Server and Windows Server 2003 for remote operating system installation, the NICs must be PXE-compliant. PXE enables the computer to contact a RIS server across the network to initiate an operating system installation.

Wireless Components

There aren't quite as many options for wireless components as there are for wired ones, but the number of wireless devices is rapidly increasing. So, the range of available options is increasing. Your first step in choosing your wireless hardware is to settle on a wireless technology.

Settling on a Technology

As explained in Chapter 2, there are three wireless standards in common use today:

▶ **802.11a** — This standard supports up to 54Mbps and operates in the uncrowded 5GHz band. Typical range is from 25-75 feet indoors. Public hotspots are generally unavailable.

▶ **802.11b** — This standard provides for up to 11Mbps data rates and is readily available. Many public hotspots support 802.11a. It operates in the relatively crowded 2.4GHz band with cordless phones and certain other devices. Typical range is from 100-150 feet indoors.

▶ **802.11g** — This standard supports up to 54Mbps and operates in the 2.4GHz band. It is backward compatible with 802.11b at 11Mbps, and G-band public hotspots are becoming much more common. It is not compatible with 802.11a. The technology has recently been expanded to support 108Mbps.

Which one is right for your network? If you have no wireless devices in place now, I recommend 802.11g. This standard provides backwards compatibility with 802.11b devices and the faster 802.11g devices. Choose one of the other standards only if you need to support A or B devices exclusively. If you need to support multiple standards in your wireless network, look for an access point that supports those standards.

Choosing Access Points

An *access point* serves as the connection between wireless devices and the wired network (whether that network contains computers or is your broadband Internet connection). Which access point you choose, and how many you deploy, depends on the wireless devices you will be using and the area in which you need to provide wireless connectivity. There are several issues to consider.

Standards

Naturally, the first consideration is the standard that the device must support—A, B, or G. Simply installing an access point doesn't guarantee fast access by all wireless users, however. If you install a 108Mbps-capable access point, the client adapters you use must also support the same enhanced G standard for them to operate at 108Mbps. In addition, factors such as interference and range will limit wireless performance.

WEP and WPA

Wired Equivalent Privacy (WEP) and Wi-Fi Protected Access (WPA) are two security features that help secure the wireless network from snooping and unauthorized access. WEP provides encryption to help secure wireless traffic. Look for a model that supports 128-bit encryption.

WPA expands on WEP to provide better security through improved encryption. WPA also supports authentication through Extensible Authentication Protocol (EAP). Support for EAP and user authentication helps ensure that only authorized users are allowed to access the wireless network. For best security, look for devices that support WPA.

Support

As with other equipment, choosing an access point from an established vendor will help ensure continued support in the future. Several manufacturers to consider include LinkSys, U.S. Robotics, 3COM, Belkin, D-Link, and Netgear.

Gateway

If you are setting up a small network with only wireless devices, or with a very small number of wired computers, a wireless access point that serves as your Internet gateway, router, and firewall could be a great all-in-one solution. Look for an access point that incorporates a built-in switch for the wired devices and can also function as a gateway router.

Coverage

Consider the area over which you want to provide wireless access to your network, taking into account building size and structure. Then factor in the expected range for your access points to determine how many you will need and where the access points should be located. Keep in mind that you will need to tie the access points to the network and your Internet gateway with cable.

Choosing Client NICs

You're not finished with the wireless network planning after you pick an access point. Each client also needs a wireless NIC. Many newer notebooks and Tablet PCs incorporate built-in wireless client hardware, eliminating the need for you to add anything to these PCs to connect them to your wireless network. You only need to configure the existing hardware to suit the configuration and settings of the access point.

If you do need to obtain wireless hardware for some of your computers, keep the following points in mind.

Form Factor

Notebooks can accommodate two types of wireless adapters: USB and PC Card. The former connects to the notebook through one of its USB ports, and the latter connects through one of the computer's PC Card slots. The PC Card format is preferable for a notebook in my opinion, because the adapter essentially becomes a part of the PC, rather than being connected to the computer by a cable that has to be connected and disconnected when you pack and unpack the computer.

Desktop computers have two options: an ISA/PCI adapter or USB. The ISA/PCI solution uses a special adapter card that installs in one of the computer's ISA or PCI slots. The card either contains the wireless hardware or contains a slot in which you insert a PC Card format wireless card. The card either includes its own antenna or provides a jack to which you connect an external antenna.

In general, I prefer USB devices for desktop computers because computers are often placed on the floor, with an internal adapter located behind the computer—often against a wall—where wireless range is reduced. A USB adapter gives you the capability to place the wireless hardware on the desktop, where interference is reduced and range generally increased. If you must use an internal card, an external antenna placed on the desk can often overcome range problems. Some PC Card adapters include a socket to support connection of an external antenna.

Compatibility and Support

I hate to repeat myself, but choose a known manufacturer with a good track record. This will help ensure availability of technical support and driver updates. Also make sure that the devices you choose will support the operating system(s) in use on your network.

> *Tech Tip:*
> Windows XP incorporates several improvements for wireless networking, making it a good upgrade option for computers currently running Windows 2000 or earlier.

Summary

Starting with the right hardware is the first step in building a reliable, useful network. There is certainly nothing wrong with putting all of your eggs in one basket and choosing a single manufacturer for all of the equipment.

Keep in mind that infrastructure devices such as racks, shelves, and patch panels are important components and will help you implement a clean, well-designed network.

Take the time to sketch your network in some fashion to plan the location of the major components, identify wireless coverage areas, and start to build an installation plan. The next chapter will help you do just that!

Building and Securing Your Network

Chapter 4

Cabling and Setting Up the Physical Network

At this point you should have your network layout well defined, at least logically if not physically. You should also have determined what equipment you will use, the network's topology, and whether wireless will be a part of the network.

Now it's time to start planning the physical network and begin the task of actually building it. Even though you might have a logical network plan at this point, you still need a physical plan. That's where we'll start.

Planning the Network

There are several considerations for building a network, all of which you should contemplate before starting the process of cabling or other installation tasks. The first of these is to decide where equipment will be located.

Locating the Equipment

In a typical small wireless network, you only need to concern yourself with the placement of an access point and perhaps a cable or DSL modem for your broadband Internet connection. When you're installing a wired network or a combined wired/wireless network, the physical layout of the network becomes much more of an issue.

First, one of the main considerations is your Internet connection, if any. Since you will likely be tying your network to the Internet, the LAN equipment should be located near your Internet connection if possible.

For example, let's assume that you have a broadband DSL connection. Your network will likely include the following:

▶   DSL Modem

▶   DSL Router

▶   Firewall

▶   Switch

In smaller networks, the router, firewall, and switch will often be integral. In larger networks, you'll likely need a separate switch to accommodate all of the devices that need to connect to the network, as well as a patch panel to simplify connections (Figure 4.1). In any case, locating all of the equipment in a wiring closet along with the broadband modem makes it easy to connect all of these devices. Placing them in a wiring closet—or at least a lockable enclosure—lets you protect the devices from accidental or intentional meddling.

Figure 4.1: A Cable Management Module Included with a Patch Panel.

If the location where your Internet connection comes into the building isn't suitable for an enclosure and you can't move the modem to a suitable location, you can simply run a cable from the modem to the broadband router. However, make sure you don't exceed the distance limits for the cable. See Chapter 3 for a discussion of racks and enclosures for your network infrastructure equipment.

Planning Cable Runs

This section offers advice on planning your cable runs. For a discussion of the best practices and common mistakes in network cabling, see the section "Running Cable— Dos and Don'ts" later in this chapter.

First, make a good survey of the building(s) to be networked and identify any potential problems, such as structural features that would make wiring difficult or impossible. Second, look for ways to run cable that are not only easy, but which provide a clean, neat installation. For example, running cable in hidden areas such as above a suspended ceiling or below a raised floor gets the cable out of sight and away from potential damage and tampering. However, you might not have either of these options available to you. Instead, you might have to run cable up or down through walls or exposed on the face of the wall.

In a nutshell, identify where devices need to be located and decide how the cables will get from the patch panel to the devices. Also consider what tools you'll need, if any, to drill through walls, floors, and otherwise run the cable.

 Caution:

Keep fire codes in mind when making any hole, whether in a floor, wall, or ceiling. Depending on the building and its use, codes might dictate that you use a fire stop of some kind. Check your local fire code to be sure.

Integrating Wired and Wireless Segments

If your network will include a wireless segment in addition to a wired segment, you should also consider where the wireless equipment will be located in relation to the wired network. If yours is a small network and you're using an access point as the switch that connects the wired devices, the access point must be located at the wiring closet or whatever central location you choose for the patch panel or Internet hardware.

If you need to locate the access point away from the wiring closet to provide better range and coverage, you'll need to include a switch at the wiring closet and run a cable from the switch to the access point(s). See Chapter 9 to learn more about integrating and configuration a wireless access point.

Running Cable—Dos and Don'ts

There is a right way and a wrong way to do most things, and sometimes we learn this the hard way. This is true when it comes to running network cables. This section offers advice and tips on how to create a neat, functional, and code-compliant network.

Tips for Pulling Cable

If you've planned ahead, you should run into relatively few problems when it comes time to start running network cables. But there are some general steps you can take to make sure the job goes as smoothly as possible:

▶ **Label each cable end** — This is an important step that will help you keep track of which cable is which. You can use a label maker or a fine-point marker to label each end of the cable. Your labels can be as simple as a certain number of dots on each end.

▶ **Use a tone generator to identify cables** — This tool consists of two components: a tone generator that clips to one end of the cable, and another device that you point at the other end of the cable, and which picks up and plays the tone through a small speaker. In effect, the tone generator sends a signal through the cable to help you locate the other end of the cable. When you point it at a cable end and it makes a noise, you know you've found the right cable end.

▶ **Pull cable from the box** — If you're pulling a lot of cable runs, you probably purchased (or should purchase) the cable in bulk. Network cable comes on a spool mounted inside a cardboard box. Leave the spool in the box and pull the cable through the hole provided for that purpose. Don't cut off as much cable as you need and then start pulling, because the cable will invariably get tangled up.

▶ **Keep cables neatly coiled and secured as you pull them** — In situations where you must work with a long length of cable, keep the cable(s) neatly coiled and use a removable hook-and-loop tape tie wrap to keep the cable from unraveling and becoming tangled. For example, if you're running a cable through a suspended ceiling, you'll probably toss the cable several feet, then move your ladder and toss the cable again. Each time, uncoil only the amount you can throw, and then secure it again before throwing it.

▶ **Pull a spare** — If you're running several cables to a particular location, pull at least one spare cable in case one of the cables turns out to be bad (occasionally a conductor will break in the cable). This is particularly good advice if the run is difficult to make—you don't want to make that run twice.

▶ **Use a fish tape** — You'll find these in home improvement and hardware stores. It's a coil of thin, narrow steel with a bent hook on one end, encased in a housing to keep it coiled. When running cable down through a wall to a receptacle, for example, you push the tape up from the receptacle to the overhead, attach the cable to the fish tape, and then pull the tape through the wall. Use the hook on the end of the tape to secure the cable to the tape while pulling. Be careful not to bend the tape too tightly or it will break.

▶ **Pull a mason's string for additional cables** — To make it easier to pull additional cables in the future, particularly when running cable through a wall, pull a length of mason's string along with one of the cables and leave a foot or so of the string inside the receptacle box and as much at the other end. When you need to run another cable, you can simply attach it securely to the string with duct tape or electrical tape, and then pull the string from the other end through to pull the cable. Make sure to attach another length of string to the cable before pulling it so you'll have a string ready for next time, if you ever need to do this again.

▶ **Use one cable to pull another** — Keep in mind that cable is relatively cheap and to some degree expendable. If you realize after the fact that you needed to pull two cables rather than one for a particular run, it might be easier to simply connect two new cables to the old one and use the original cable to pull the two new ones. You can also use this solution when you run a cable and discover that it is bad—just hook another to the end of it and pull it through.

▶ **Tape tips** — When you pull more than one cable at a time, it's a good bet you'll use electrical tape or duct tape to bundle the cables together. Here's an electrician's trick: fold over the last bit of tape so that it sticks to itself, rather than just wrapping it around the cable. You'll then be able to remove the tape much more easily. This is also a good method to use when taping wire nuts for house wiring.

▶ **Use lubricant** — When pulling cable through conduit, use a cable lubricant to help the cable slide easily through the conduit, around 90-degree bends, and so on. Check with your cable provider for a recommended lubricant, or check `www.gmptools.com`, `www.polywater.com`, or perform an online search on the term "cable lubricant".

What to Avoid

Just as there are certain things you can do to make pulling cables easier, there are things to avoid:

▶ **Don't run cable where it doesn't belong** — For safety and the longevity of the cable, don't run cable in places where it shouldn't be. For example, don't run it under a carpet where it will be walked on and eventually damaged. It's acceptable to run cable right along the perimeter of the wall, tucked between the baseboard and the carpet—just make sure the cable isn't under the carpet where a piece of furniture might crimp and eventually damage it. Also, don't run non-plenum cable in a plenum area.

▶ **Electrical cables** — Avoid running network cables near electrical wiring because the electrical field created by the electrical wiring can cause performance problems. If you must run network cable near electrical wiring, make the cables cross at as close to a right angle as possible.

▶ **Light fixtures and other equipment** — Avoid fluorescent light fixtures when running cable if at all possible. Run the cable around the fixture at least two feet away, rather than over the fixture. Also avoid running cable near heavy equipment and devices with large electric motors or pumps.

▶ **Too little cable slack** — Cables must have some slack to prevent damage to the cable. It's better to leave too much slack than not enough. Leave the cable relatively loose (don't pull it tight) and leave a service loop of at least a couple of feet at the wiring closet.

▶ **Long bend radii** — When bending cable, use a long radius (don't bend the cable too tightly). Using too tight a bend radius can crimp the wire and potentially break one or more conductors. This advice is particularly important when running fiber optic cable.

▶ **Protect the cable** — This goes hand-in-hand with not running the cable where it shouldn't be. Don't run cable near heat sources, where it can be stepped on or caught by someone walking by, or in other locations where the cable can be easily damaged. If you run exposed cable, use raceway to protect and hide the cable.

Making a Clean and Code-Compliant Installation

Your local and state building codes will have an impact on how you wire your network, assuming you want to make the effort to comply. No one is likely to inspect your wiring for a home network, but that doesn't mean you shouldn't try to comply with all applicable codes. If you have a fire, for example, you won't want to be in the situation of having used non-plenum cable in a plenum space (see Chapter 3 for more details). There might certainly be a liability or insurance issue, but more important, it's simply a safety hazard.

An office network is a different situation. If the Fire Marshall checks your wiring and finds that you've suspended cables from your sprinkler system, you could end up rewiring your network. It doesn't hurt to check with your local building inspector and fire marshal to learn about any specific requirements for wiring in your locale.

In addition, if you want to ensure that your cabling is up to code and you're willing to spend the research time, take a trip to www.bicsi.org. Click the **Publications** link and choose **Cabling Installation**. The *Information Transport Systems Installation Manual* covers installation requirements and practices to achieve a code- and standards-compliant installation.

Here are a few tips for making a clean and neat installation:

▶ **Check codes beforehand** — Before you run the first cable, take the time to determine what codes apply to your installation and follow them.

▶ **Keep cable organized** — Try not to run cable so that the cables twist around one another. This will make it easier to identify cables and simplify the prospect of replacing cables in the future.

▶ **Use raceway for exposed cable** — Raceway not only protects the cable, but organizes and hides it for a neater appearance.

▶ **Use receptacles** — Definitely use receptacles for cables that come through the wall, but also use surface-mounted receptacles for cables laid through raceway.

▶ **Use ties** — Coil slack at the wiring closet and secure with cable ties. Plastic ties work well, as do hook-and-loop tape ties. Also use ties to secure cables to the rack, as discussed in the next section.

If you decide that you simply don't want the hassle of running cables, contact a local contractor or networking consultant about running the cable for you. Choose a company that provides certified cabling installers. You can still perform the remainder of the network setup and configuration yourself after the cable has been pulled.

Setting Up the Wiring Closet

In a home network, it's likely that you have no wiring closet but instead will be locating your networking equipment next to the phone or cable connection where the broadband modem is located. That might be in your living room, home office, or even bedroom. If you're adding wiring to several rooms, it might make sense to place the switch, patch panel, and other infrastructure equipment in the basement, a closet, or other area that is either centrally located or just out of the way and out of sight. If you don't want to move the broadband connection or equipment, you can simply run a cable from it to your DSL router or switch.

For a business network, I recommend setting up the equipment in an unused room or storage area that can be locked. The location where your phone service enters the building could be a good location. The key is that the equipment should be located in an area that is not accessible to the public or to your employees, with the exception of those who will administer the network.

Tech Tip:

In one of the businesses I co-owned, we framed two glass patio doors into a corner of one of the offices to create a server room or wiring center (as shown in Figure 4.2). The glass enabled us to keep an eye on the equipment and who was using it, and the locks on the doors kept everyone honest. We routed an air conditioning duct to the suspended ceiling over our makeshift server room for cooling. It wasn't the best solution, but it worked well for our purposes and fit in the budget. Just keep in mind that you can create a professional-looking and functional closet with relatively little expense.

Figure 4.2: Server Room Built by Framing Two Glass Patio Doors in One Corner of an Office.

The first step in setting up the wiring closet is to prepare the area that will hold the equipment. For a home network, this might mean simply mounting a shelf to the wall or clearing off one corner of your desktop. In a larger network, preparing the area could mean mounting the rack or enclosure that will house the equipment. If you choose a floor-standing rack, make sure to mount it securely to the floor with appropriate bolts. For a cement subfloor, drill holes in the cement and use anchor bolts to secure the rack. For wood subfloors, lag bolts are the ticket. Wall-mounted racks should be securely mounted to wall studs. Toggle bolts can be used where studs aren't available, but this isn't the ideal method. A better alternative is to mount a sheet of 3/4" plywood to the wall, secured to the studs, and then mount the rack to the plywood.

After the rack is mounted, it should be grounded. To meet code, you must use a ground wire of not less than 14 gauge and not greater than 6 gauge to an earthen ground—a ground rod driven into the ground. You can't use plumbing to ground the rack, nor can you simply tie into the ground wire for an electrical circuit. If you're not comfortable doing this part of the job, hire an electrician to make the ground connection for you.

Note:

The National Electrical Code (NEC) specifies that the ground wire have a current-carrying capacity approximately equal to that of the grounded metallic member(s) and protected conductor(s). Again, have an electrician make the ground if you're not comfortable doing so.

Tech Tip:

If you intend to use the wiring closet for a server room, consider installing antistatic flooring in the room. At a minimum, install a grounding mat in front of the server and make sure the mat is grounded (either to the grounded rack or to the ground itself).

Terminating Cables and Making Connections

After the cables are run, it's time to start making connections. A little care and a little extra effort will ensure a trouble-free and professional-looking installation. Let's take a look at some key points.

Using Patch Panels and Other Installation Hardware

First, unless you are setting up a small network with—at most—three or four computers, don't terminate the cables with connectors and simply plug them into the switch. Instead, install a patch panel (see Chapter 3 for more details). The patch panel should be secured to the rack or enclosure, if used.

The location of the patch panel in relation to where the cables enter the wiring closet isn't very important. What is important is the location of the patch panel relative to the rest of the equipment—particularly the switch. The cables can be bundled and attached to one side of the rack or enclosure frame to route them neatly to the patch panel and not conflict with the other devices (Figure 4.3). However, the patch cables will connect from the patch panel to the switch, and patch cables will also run from the other devices (router, firewall, etc.) to the switch, all from the front of the rack. So, locate the patch panel in relation to the switch such that the patch cables you use will reach and can be neatly routed between the two. Use cable management units where appropriate to organize and secure the patch cables.

Figure 4.3: Route and Attach Cables to the Rack to Secure Them Neatly Out of the Way.

Tech Tip:

In some cases you might want to mount a device to the back side of the front rack frame rather than the front side. The switch and patch panel in Figure 4.3 are mounted rearward to keep the patch cables inside the front frame of the rack. The reason for doing so in this particular installation was an access trapdoor to the attic that was located above and in front of the rack. The door would have hit the cables if the switch and panel had been installed fully forward.

Also make sure to support the cables. They should not be suspended by their punch-down connections on the patch panel. Instead, attach the cables to the rack or enclosure with wire ties to relieve any strain on the punch-connections (see Figure 4.4). Then, route them to the patch panel for connection.

Figure 4.4: Attach the Cables to the Rack for Strain Relief.

Making Cable Terminations

Chapter 3 suggested that you use patch panels and pre-manufactured patch cables to simplify and reduce the number of cable terminations you have to make. Even so, you must make some terminations. For example, you need to punch down the cables to the back of the patch panel and receptacle modules. You might also need to make a few cables or crimp connectors on a few cables.

First, you should follow termination standards for RJ45 connections. You could simply connect the individual conductors in a twisted-pair cable in any way you wanted to the connector, assuming you connected the other end of the cable in the same way. However, there are standards for terminating cables. In fact, there are two primary standards: EIA/TIA 568/A and EIA/TIA 568/B. Table 4.1 illustrates the color/pin combinations for each standard.

> *Note:*
>
> Here's how to locate pin 1. Hold the RJ45 connector with the little retainer clip facing down and the cable facing toward you. You should be looking at the side of the connector where the conductors are visible. Pin 1 is at the left, as shown in Figure 4.5.

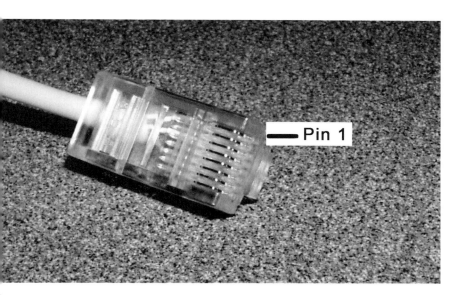

Figure 4.5: Pin 1 on an RJ45 Connector.

Pin #	EIA/TIA 568/A	EIA/TIA 568/A
1	White/Green	White/Orange
2	Green/White	Orange/White
3	White/Orange	White/Green
4	Blue/White	Blue/White
5	White/Blue	White/Blue
6	Orange/White	Green/White
7	White/Brown	White/Brown
8	Brown/White	Brown/White

Table 4.1: EIA/TIA Cable Termination Standards.

Note:

In the color designations in Table 4.1, colors starting with a color other than white can also be a solid color. For example, a wire designated Green / White in Table 4.1 could actually be solid green without any white. Wire designations that start with "White" are always striped with white and the other color.

You need to follow some standard to ensure that the cables are terminated properly, so you might as well follow an accepted and industry-recognized standard. Generally, the 568/B standard is used, but you can use the older 568/A standard, as well. Just be consistent and use the same standard throughout.

> **Note:**
>
> The main reason to use the 568/A standard is if you already have some older network infrastructure in place that uses the A standard and want to ensure consistency throughout the network. 568/A maintains blue pair compatibility with telco (telephone) connections.

When punching down connections to patch panels and jack modules, you'll find that these items typically provide color-coding to make connections easier. You can simply match up the colors and punch them down without thinking much about it. However, understand that the panel or module likely provides color coding for both the 568/A and 568/B standards. Make sure you match the wire colors to the appropriate posts on the panel or module according to the standard you are using (see Figure 4.6).

Figure 4.6: Color-Coded Connections on the Back of a Patch Panel.

Make sure to follow the appropriate standard when punching connections to the patch panel.

Now it's time to start making some connections. The twisted-pair cable includes a sheath that retains, protects, and helps insulate the twisted pairs. You can buy a stripper to remove the sheath, but in a small installation it is typical to use wire cutters. That's the approach taken here.

Note:

Be careful not to knick or cut the insulation on the twisted pairs. Do not strip any of the insulation from the pairs, either.

To make a termination, first cut the cable with wire cutters. Then, snip the insulation lengthwise with the cutters about half an inch or so. Look for the zip string inside the sheath and pull the string down through the slit to split the sheath further. With a few inches of wire pairs exposed, remove the excess sheath with the cutter. Now you're ready to start making the connection.

Here are some additional tips on making those connections:

▶ **Don't untwist pairs** — As explained in previous chapters, the pairs in a twisted-pair cable are twisted for a reason—to reduce crosstalk. If you untwist the pairs, you lose the benefit of the twist and introduce the possibility of crosstalk. When making cable terminations, whether to a patch panel or an RJ45 connector, only untwist the absolute minimum needed to make the connection.

▶ **Use the right tool for the job** — You can do most small wiring jobs with wire cutters and a punch-down tool. Check at your local home improvement store or other location where you purchase the cable and other infrastructure items for a sheath stripper and RJ45 crimper, if you want to use them. The stripper is optional; the crimper is required if you intend to make any RJ45 terminations.

▶ **Pay attention to the orientation of the punch-down tool and use extra wire** — The punch-down tool serves two purposes. It seats the wire in the posts and also cuts the extra wire as you punch it down. Look at the end of the tool to determine which side is the cutter, and make sure to face that edge of the tool to the side of the post where the excess wire needs to be cut off. Since the tool cuts the wire, you can place an extra inch or two over the post as needed before you punch it down.

Tech Tip:

Don't untwist the wire before you punch it down. Instead, separate the conductors in the pair an inch or two back from the end of the wired, as shown in Figure 4.7. Separate the two just enough to reach their two separate posts, then punch them down. The tool will cut off the excess.

Figure 4.7: Untwist Only Enough Wire to Punch Down the Connection.

▶ **Support modules when punching connections** — When punching connections to the patch panel, a swing-out rack or access from the back of the rack makes the job much easier. You can mount the patch panel, and then either swing open the rack or work from behind it to punch down the wires. If you can't get behind it, flip the patch panel 180 degrees toward you and temporarily mount it backwards and upside down in the rack. Punch down the wires, then remove the screws and reinstall the panel with the wire terminations to the rear. When terminating a cable to a module for a receptacle, run the cable out of the receptacle, hold the module in place backwards on its mounting plate, punch down the wire, and then install the module.

► **Use properly rated connectors** — Make sure to use Cat5-rated modules for Cat5 cable installations and Cat6-rated modules for Cat6 installations.

Crossover Cables

To this point the discussion has focused on straight cables, where the wire runs from the same pin on each end of the cable (such as from pin 2 on one end to pin 2 at the other). Sometimes, however, a *crossover* cable is needed. For example, you might need to use a crossover cable between the broadband modem and the router. Crossover cables are also used to connect two switches, hubs, or transceivers. Essentially, the cable crosses the transmit and receive lines so the two devices can talk to each other—kind of like holding two telephone handsets speaker-to-microphone.

Tech Tip:
You can network two computers with a crossover cable (assuming a NIC in each one) and eliminate the switch or hub between them.

Tables 4.2 and 4.3 show the pin and color combinations for a crossover cable.

Pin #	One End (568/B)	Other End (568/B)
1	White/Orange	White/Green
2	Orange/White	Green/White
3	White/Green	White/Orange
4	Blue/White	Blue/White
5	White/Blue	White/Blue
6	Green/White	Orange/White
7	White/Brown	White/Brown
8	Brown/White	Brown/White

Table 4.2: EIA/TIA 568/B Cable Termination for a Crossover Cable.

Pin #	One End (568/A)	Other End (568/A)
1	White/Green	White/Orange
2	Green/White	Orange/White
3	White/Orange	White/Green
4	Blue/White	Blue/White
5	White/Blue	White/Blue
6	Orange/White	Green/White
7	White/Brown	White/Brown
8	Brown/White	Brown/White

Table 4.3: EIA/TIA 568/B Cable Termination for a Crossover Cable.

How to Make a Clean Installation

As noted earlier in this chapter, there is a right way and a wrong way to build a network. Doing it right includes making sure your installation is organized and neat. Obviously, the neater the installation, the better it looks.

Looks have nothing to do with function, however. A rat's nest of wiring will function as well as a neatly organized one. The difference comes when you need to work on the network to troubleshoot or expand it. The more orderly the installation, the easier it will be for you to locate specific cables and simply work around the cables to access the router, firewall, and so on.

The first bit of advice I offer is to use care and organization when you run the cables. Route cables along the edge of the rack (enclosure) and use cable ties to bind them to it. Where lots of cables are involved, a wire management panel can help organize the cables across the face of the rack.

In addition to organizing the cable, also label the patch panel and cables if possible to help you quickly identify what is connected at the other end. It's also a good idea to label the firewall, router, and other devices with their global IP settings. However, if equipment is visible to non-administrators, the labeling should be placed on the bottom of the device, out of sight. In addition, never post or label authentication information for devices.

You should document the network when it is finished. Include in the diagram the logical connection between devices, the IP address information for each device, DHCP information, and other pertinent data. This will help you or other technicians in the future quickly identify network settings when troubleshooting or expanding the network.

Summary

This chapter explained the finer points of planning and executing your network infrastructure installation. A good layout starts with a neat installation at the wiring closet or other central location for the router, firewall, and other equipment, and moves out from there.

Pay attention to building codes when you are running cable to make sure you don't run afoul of the Fire Marshall. Not only could you open yourself up to some liability, but you might end up having to re-cable the network.

Take the time during installation to neatly route and secure the cables. A neat installation not only looks better and certainly more professional, but will make it easier to troubleshoot and expand the network when the time comes.

Did you know?

Failing to ground an equipment rack could eventually result in damage to devices mounted in the rack due to static buildup.

Chapter 5

Configuring Your Internet Connection

After the network infrastructure is in place, the next step is to make sure your Internet connection, if there is one, is configured and ready for the network tie-in. This chapter explains the topics related to configuring the Internet connection and making the network Internet-ready. Here you learn about setting up dial-up connections (if you plan to share a dial-up with others), configuring the network's router, and setting up port forwarding. All of these tasks require an understanding of TCP/IP and related services, so that's where we'll start.

Understanding and Configuring TCP/IP

TCP/IP stands for Transmission Control Protocol / Internet Protocol. TCP/IP is a suite of protocols by which Internet traffic flows. This section provides an overview of TCP/IP and also explains how to configure various aspects of TCP/IP.

First, TCP/IP isn't a single protocol. Rather, it is a group of protocols. For example, IP is the protocol that enables computers to communicate with one another. TCP is the protocol that ensures the IP packets are sent and received properly. The following are some of the protocols in the TCP/IP suite:

▶ Address Resolution Protocol (ARP)

▶ Internet Control Message Protocol (ICMP)

▶ Internet Group Management Protocol (IGMP)

▶ Internet Protocol (IP)

▶ Transmission Control Protocol (TCP)

Second, TCP/IP might not be the only network protocol you use on your network. For example, computers running Windows that also need to communicate with a Mac server or Mac-hosted printer might also run the AppleTalk protocol.

In the past, Windows networks often used the NetBEUI protocol for local area network sharing and TCP/IP for Internet access. With the introduction of Windows 2000, Microsoft made TCP/IP the default protocol. When you install Windows XP for example, Setup automatically adds and configures TCP/IP on the computer. So, you can use TCP/IP as the only protocol to support both LAN sharing and Internet access. However, you should make sure that your LAN is protected from the Internet by a firewall. See Chapter 6 for more details on firewalls and security.

Now, let's take a look at specific TCP/IP topics you'll need to know before you set up your network and Internet connection.

DHCP and IP Addressing

Each device in an IP network is assigned an IP address that uniquely identifies the device. In a way, an IP address is like a house's street address that tells people how to get to the house. The IP address tells other computers how to send traffic to your computer. A network can't contain two devices with the same address—every device must have a unique address.

The IP addressing standard I'll focus on in this book is the IPv4 standard, which is used by default for all Windows computers, as well as Linux-based systems, Macintosh, and others. An IPv4 address is a 32-bit address organized into four eight-bit *octets* separated by periods, like this one: 192.168.1.100.

In addition to an address, a *subnet mask* is assigned to each device. A subnet is a division of an IP network where all devices share the same IP address prefixes. A small network, for example, might use the IP address range 192.168.0.n, where n varies from 1 to 254. This range represents what is called a Class C network address range. It is identified by the subnet mask 255.255.255.0. As you can see from this example, the subnet mask is a 32-bit value just like the IP address, and is also written as four octets separated by periods.

When a device prepares to send an IP data packet, it checks the address against the subnet mask to determine if the destination address resides on the same subnet. If they are on the same subnet, the device uses ARP to determine the destination node's MAC address (its physical hardware address) and sends the packet directly. If they are not on the same subnet, ARP determines the next hop and the packet is sent to the default gateway defined in the local device's network settings.

What does all of this mean to you? Basically, every device will have not only an IP address but also a subnet mask. The IP address will differ but the subnet mask will be the same for all devices on a given subnet. Most small networks use a single subnet. The exception is a network containing a wireless access point and a wired network segment. Often, the wireless devices reside on one subnet and the wired devices reside on another. Figure 5.1 illustrates such a network. In addition, many wireless access modes can run in bridge mode, enabling them to reside on the wired network's subnet. This latter option simplifies file and printer sharing between wireless and wired devices. A third option is to configure the wireless access point as a router and disable its internal firewall, enabling resource sharing traffic to pass through in both directions. Not all access points support this configuration, however. See the section "Choosing a Subnet for the Network" later in this chapter for details on how to pick the address range for your network.

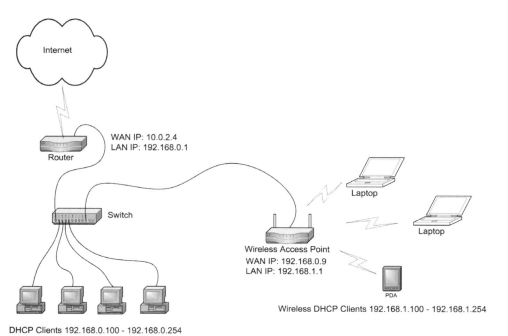

Figure 5.1: Small Network Incorporating Two Subnets.

Public Versus Private Addresses

A public address is one that resides in the public Internet address space. Public addresses are managed and allocated by the regional registries such as ARIN, RIPE, and AfnNIC, which allocate them to large Internet providers, which further allocate them to their downstream ISP customers. (These regional registries are governed by IANA, the Internet Assigned Numbers Authority.) The ISP then allocates a certain number of addresses to you. This means you can't simply pick a range of public IP addresses to use for your LAN's external interface to the Internet. Instead, the address or addresses must be assigned to you by your service provider.

Private IP address ranges are set aside for networks that are not connected to the Internet or which are connected to the Internet by a device (such as a router) that hides the network from the Internet. These addresses take the same form as public IP addresses. The only difference is that the IANA has set aside these ranges and private address ranges:

10.0.0.0 through 10.255.255.255
172.16.0.0 through 172.31.255.255
192.168.0.0 through 192.168.255.255

These address ranges are not routable, and therefore can be used by multiple organizations. For example, you might pick 192.168.1.n for your LAN and the company next door might do the same. There is no conflict because the two networks are separate from one another. However, keep in mind that connecting a private subnet range to the Internet requires a router that performs Network Address Translation, or NAT. To the outside world the private subnet is identified by one or more public IP addresses. The router takes care of translating the addresses public-to-private and vice-versa.

How many public IP addresses do you need? If you will not be running any servers on your network, you need only one. You can also get by with one even if you host servers on the network, provided you only host one for each port assignment. For example, HTTP uses port 80. You can host one HTTP (Web) server with a single public IP address. This one server can host multiple Web sites, each with a different host header but all with the same port assignment of 80. If you add a second server to the network that will use port 80, you need a second public IP address.

Also understand that you can host multiple services on one physical server or split the services up among multiple servers. So, you might have one Web server and one mail server, or both services might be hosted on a single computer.

Bottom line: you need one public IP address for each instance of a given port number hosted on the LAN. Two servers running port 80 services, for example, require two public IP addresses, but those servers can host other services and ports.

Choosing a Subnet for the Network

It's most likely that you will use a private subnet for your LAN. There is no reason not to do so as long as your router performs NAT. You can then use a small number of public addresses for the external side of the router as assigned by your provider.

Which subnet should you choose? It really doesn't matter. Simply pick an address range that accommodates the number of devices on your network. For example, you might choose 192.168.0.0 and a subnet mask of 255.255.255.0 to accommodate up to 254 devices. Many SOHO routers default to a LAN subnet of 192.168.1.0 / 255.255.255.0, and that's a perfectly good choice as well.

Assigning IP Addresses

The IP address can be assigned in more than one way. First, you can specify the address statically by configuring the computer for a specific IP address and subnet mask, as shown in Figure 5.2. With static addressing, a device's address remains constant unless you change it.

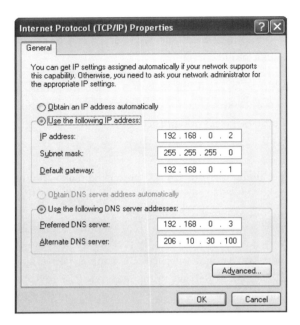

Figure 5.2: You Can Assign the Computer's IP Address Dynamically or Statically.

Note:

This chapter doesn't cover client TCP/IP configuration. See Chapter 7 to learn how to set up clients' addressing and other TCP/IP settings.

Static addressing offers the advantage of not requiring a device to assign addresses automatically. However, managing the address space becomes more difficult as the number of devices increases. For example, it's easy to manage the network address space for 10 computers, but managing the addresses for 50 would become a chore. That's where DHCP comes into play.

DHCP stands for Dynamic Host Configuration Protocol. DHCP provides the mechanism for a DHCP server to automatically assign IP addresses and related IP settings to computers on the network. After you configure the DHCP server, the computers can pull their IP settings dynamically from the server each time they boot. When you configure a computer to receive its address automatically, you're configuring it for DHCP, as shown in Figure 5.3.

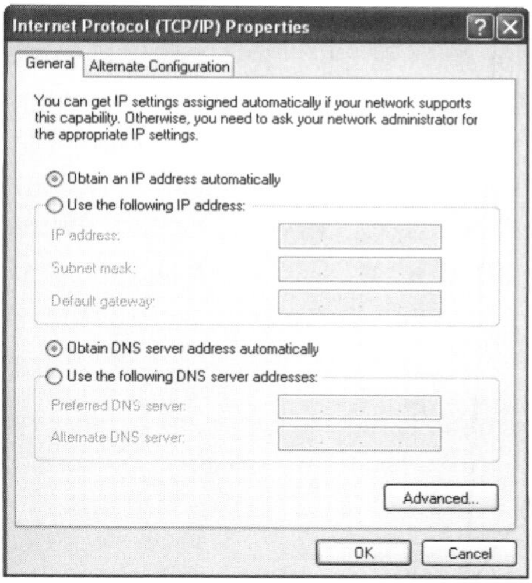

Figure 5.3: Computer Configured for DHCP.

In most small networks you don't need a computer on the network to function as a DHCP server. Instead, the router, firewall, or access point will function as a DHCP server. In my own home network, for example, the NETGEAR firewall functions as the DHCP server (See Figure 5.4). See the section "Using APIPA for Networks Without an Internet Connection" later in this chapter to learn about an alternative to DHCP.

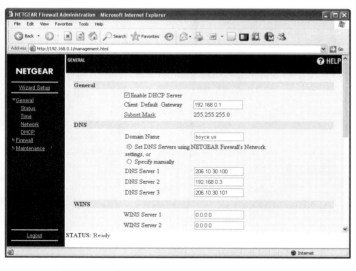

Figure 5.4: NETGEAR Firewall Functioning as a DHCP Server.

If you have no such device on the network that will provide DHCP support, or you don't want to use that device for that purpose, you can install a server to provide DHCP services. For example, Windows Server includes a DHCP service, as does Linux. If you're not into Linux and don't want the added expense of Windows Server, you can turn to a third-party application like Simple DNS Plus (www.jhsoft.com), which runs on all Windows platforms (such as Windows XP) and provides both DNS and DHCP services for the network. Perform a search of your favorite download site to find other DHCP server software. I've used Simple DNS Plus in the past and like the program. It is inexpensive and performs well.

The steps for setting up a DHCP server vary according to the device hosting the service. However, most of the concepts are the same across all devices. In a nutshell, you need to decide on the following:

▶ **Address range** — Determine how many devices on the network will require dynamic addressing and decide on an address range that will accommodate the devices. Plan for some growth in the range. For example, if you need to network 10 computers now, you might specify a range of 25 addresses for DHCP, such as 192.168.0.10 through 192.168.0.34.

Note:

It's a generally accepted practice to assign the first IP address in a given subnet to the gateway device. For example, if your network uses 192.168.0.n, the gateway should be 192.168.0.1. I usually leave the next several addresses unassigned to make them available for servers and other devices that require a static address. For example, the first server might be 192.168.0.2, the next 192.168.0.3, and so on.

▶ **Subnet mask** — The DHCP server assigns the subnet mask to the clients along with the IP address. Determine the subnet mask (usually 255.255.255.0 for a small network) before beginning the DHCP configuration. For more details, see the section "Choosing a Subnet for the Network," later in this chapter.

▶ **Default gateway address** — The DHCP server assigns the default gateway to the devices as well as the address and subnet mask. Determine the address that will be or is assigned to the router before configuring DHCP.

▶ **DNS server addresses** — DNS supports name-to-address mapping as explained in the section "DNS and Dynamic DNS," later in this chapter. The DHCP clients can take their DNS server settings from the DHCP server or you can assign the DNS server settings statically. I recommend that you assign them dynamically through DHCP to reduce time and administrative overhead.

▶ **Excluded addresses** — Some DHCP servers allow you to specify one or more addresses to be excluded from a DHCP range. For example, if you have network printers on the network, it's necessary to assign them static addresses rather than dynamic ones so that printing clients can find them. You can use an address that would otherwise fall inside a DHCP range if you exclude that address from the DHCP scope. DHCP will not assign the excluded address to any device.

Tech Tip:

If you can't define exclusions in your DHCP server, simply use a subset of the available subnet addresses for the range. In the 192.168.0.n subnet, for example, use 192.168.0.1 through 192.168.0.99 for the gateway, servers, printers, and other static devices, and use 192.168.0.100 through 192.168.0.254 for the DHCP range.

Now, what happens when a client that is configured for DHCP boots? Does it get a different address every time? The short answer is no. But there is no guarantee that a dynamically assigned address will be given to the same computer all the time. The DHCP address scope includes a *lease period* that determines how long the computer will retain the address. When the lease runs out, the client computer must renew the lease. Often, the DHCP server assigns the same address to the client. However, it's entirely possible that a different address might be assigned. In a small network, the DHCP lease period isn't a major issue. In fact, many devices with integrated DHCP servers do not let you change the lease period.

Using APIPA for Networks without an Internet Connection

APIPA stands for Automatic Private IP Addressing. APIPA is a feature built into Windows 2000 and later that enables a computer to choose a private address for a specific pool in cases where no DHCP server is available. APIPA uses the address range 169.254.0.1 to 169.254.255.254 with a subnet mask of 255.255.0.0.

APIPA simplifies TCP/IP use for small networks. If the computer is configured for dynamic addressing (the default) and it finds no DHCP server at startup, the computer assigns itself an APIPA address. Other computers on the network do the same. The result is that all of the computers on the LAN automatically take their addresses from the same subnet and communicate with one another without any TCP/IP configuration. It's a great option for LANs with no Internet connection because it requires no work to set up.

DNS and Dynamic DNS

The Domain Name System (DNS) provides name-to-address mapping for IP clients. For example, when you type www.boyce.us in your Web browser, the DNS resolver client built into your operating system looks up www.boyce.us to determine the IP address associated with the *www* host name. The browser then uses the resulting IP address to connect to the server and display the Web site.

There are two situations in which you'll need DNS in a small network. The first is when the network connects to the Internet and clients on the LAN will be using Internet resources such as mail servers and Web servers. The second situation is when you have applications or services on your LAN that use host names to find and access resources on the LAN.

Note:

You don't need to install a DNS server to enable your computers to share resources such as folders and printers on the LAN.

In the former situation, your ISP will provide DNS services for you and give you a list of DNS servers to enter in your client configuration. In the latter, you will need to install a DNS server inside your LAN for local name resolution. In either case, you must specify the DNS servers in your client configuration.

You can configure the DNS server addresses statically in the properties for the TCP/IP protocol on each computer, or dynamically through DHCP. If you are using dynamic addressing and DHCP, enter the DNS server addresses in the DHCP server. Otherwise, open the properties for the LAN connection on each computer and specify the DNS settings manually. See Chapter 7 to learn how to configure network settings at the client computer.

Dynamic DNS (DDNS)

Windows 2000 Server introduced a featured called Dynamic DNS, or DDNS. With DDNS, client computers can request an update of their host and pointer records in a Windows 2000 or Windows 2003 DNS server. The result is that even when the client computers' IP addresses change through DHCP, the host record can remain updated. So, DDNS enables host name resolution for client computers that are served by DHCP.

DDNS is supported at the server by Windows 2000 Server and Windows Server 2003. Computers running Windows 2000 or later can request that their host records be updated. The DNS Service in Windows 2000 Server and Windows Server can also update the host records of other client operating systems, enabling them to participate in DDNS.

Gateways

The *gateway* is the device on the LAN that serves as a connection point to the next segment on the network. In most small networks, the gateway is the connection point between the LAN and the Internet. Most often, the gateway is LAN's router. If you are using Internet Connection Sharing in Windows to share a dial-up connection or broadband Internet connection, the gateway is the computer running ICS. The ICS computer functions as the LAN's router. See Chapter 2 for a general discussion of ICS. See the section "Sharing a Broadband Connection" later in this chapter for details on using ICS.

In all cases, the gateway IP address is the LAN-side address of the router. Each client computer must be configured for at least one gateway address. As with the DNS settings, you can assign the gateway address automatically through DHCP or manually by editing the settings at each computer.

Configuring the Router

Now that you're up to speed on TCP/IP, you have the information you need to configure your router. Because this book focuses on small and home networks, it's likely that you are using a relatively inexpensive router, such as a DSL/cable router, that is configured through a set of Web pages. If that isn't the case, check with your service provider or router vendor for help in configuring the router. If your network is self-contained and does not connect to the Internet or any other network, you do not need a router.

Static Routing Versus Dynamic Routing Protocols

Routers use a *routing table* to maintain the list of routes by which packets are sent. In almost every case, you won't need to worry about routing tables and route configuration for a small network. However, I offer some coverage here in case you do need to do so for your router.

The routing table is built in one of two ways: statically or dynamically. Setting up a router to use dynamic routing is actually fairly simple. You only need to choose which routing protocol the router should use to communicate with adjacent routers. In most cases, Routing Information Protocol (RIP) is the protocol of choice. Generally speaking, you can set the routing protocol, reboot the router, and it will begin building its routing table from adjacent routers.

If you use static routing, you must add a route for each subnet to be routed through the router. A route comprises three pieces of information:

▶ **Destination address** — This address specifies the subnet for the destination to be routed. The router examines the destination address in each packet to determine which route to use to forward the packet.

▶ **Subnet mask** — This is the subnet mask of the destination subnet.

▶ **Next hop** — This is the IP address of the router that serves the subnet.

Figure 5.5 illustrates a route. In the figure, the network behind router A is your network. The other routers in the routing group represent other networks. Routes are shown for each of the other networks. As Figure 5.5 illustrates, the next hop is the IP address of the interface on the adjacent router that is in the same subnet as the WAN side of your router.

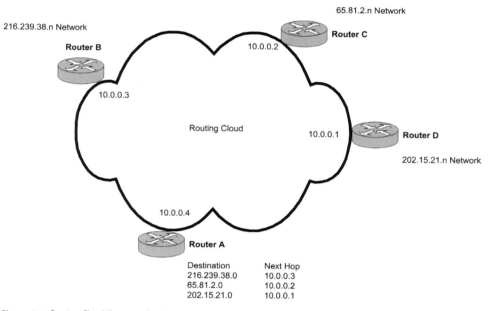

Figure 5.5: Routing Cloud Illustrates the Next Hop Values for Three Static Routes.

In addition to a route for each specific network, a router must include a *default route*. This route specifies the route to be used for all traffic not handled by any other route. The default route has a destination address of 0.0.0.0. Any traffic not destined for a specific route is sent to the next hop specified in the default route.

In most SOHO networks, you don't need to configure routes because there are no adjacent routers beyond your own other than your ISP's router. In other words, the default route that the router creates automatically based on its WAN gateway and LAN addresses is used for all packets. You only need to worry about creating routes if you are using static routing and there is more than one router adjacent to your own.

Setting the LAN and WAN Addresses

Your router lives on two subnets: your own, and your Internet service provider's subnet. Your subnet is the LAN side of the router, and the ISP's subnet is the WAN side. When you configure a router, you must specify the following:

▶ **LAN IP address and subnet mask** — Choose an unused IP address from your local subnet. It's common practice to use the first address in a subnet for the router, such as 192.168.1.1. Specify a subnet mask that matches the one in use on your LAN.

▶ **WAN IP address and subnet mask** — This is the public IP address assigned to you by your provider. Note that the assigned address might actually be a private address, depending on how the ISP has structured its network.

▶ **WAN gateway IP address** — This is the gateway address of the ISP's network. It tells your router where to direct outgoing packets. It's assigned by your ISP.

Figure 5.6 shows the configuration page for a Linksys access point router, and Figure 5.7 shows the configuration page for a NETGEAR FR314 firewall. These figures illustrate the similarity in configuration between various broadband routers/firewalls.

Figure 5.6: LinkSys Access Point Configuration Page.

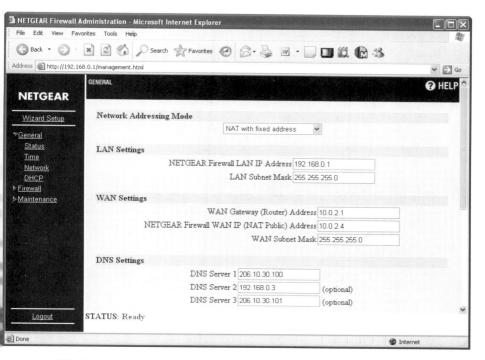

Figure 5.7: NETGEAR Firewall Configuration Page.

Configuring Port Forwarding

Another configuration issue to consider when setting up your router is *port forwarding*. This feature enables a router to identify packets that are destined for a specific port and forward them to a specific IP address on the LAN. For example, port 80 traffic might get directed to your Web server, ports 25 and 110 would get forwarded to your mail server, and so on.

If you are not hosting any servers on your LAN, it's unlikely that you need to set up port forwarding. However, you need to configure forwarding if you want to forward certain types of traffic to specific computers. For example, perhaps you want to enable an incoming Remote Desktop Connection to enable users on the network to use their computers remotely. Or maybe you want to play an Internet game that requires a specific port to be forwarded to your computer. Whatever the case, setting up port forwarding is as simple as associating a specific port with a specific internal LAN address.

Some routers make this process easier than others. Figure 5.8 shows the Port Forwarding page for a LinkSys wireless access point. For this router, you specify the external port range (which can be a single port or a range of ports), the protocol (UDP or TCP), the internal LAN address, and whether the rule is enabled. If enabled, the traffic is forwarded. If disabled, the traffic is not forwarded.

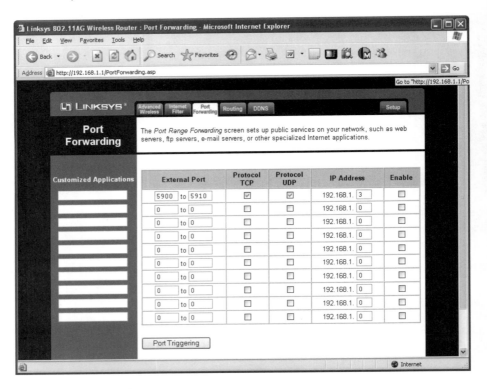

Figure 5.8: Port Forwarding Settings.

Figure 5.9 shows the port forwarding pages for a Netgear router. With this device, you must first create a named service associated with a port or range of ports, and then forward that named service to an IP address.

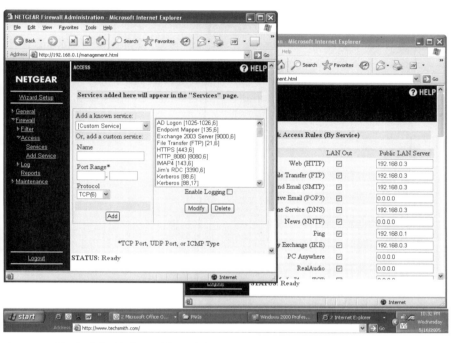

Figure 5.9: A Service Defined by Port and Forwarded.

Keep in mind that port forwarding sends *all* traffic destined for the specified port to the assigned IP address. If you need to send the same service traffic to two or more addresses, you'll have to either use a unique public IP address for each computer that requires forwarding, or use different ports for the service on each computer. For example, Remote Desktop Connection by default uses port 3389. To support RDC for three computers on a LAN with a single public IP address, you have to use three different ports, such as 3389, 3390, and 3391, each forwarded to a particular address. Plus, RDC would have to be configured on each of those computers to respond on that address.

Tech Tip:

To change the RDC listening port, see *Windows XP Power Productivity*, **Sybex, 2005. You'll also find a discussion at** http://support.microsoft.com/kb/306759.

Using Port Triggering

Port triggering is similar to port forwarding, except the outgoing and incoming ports differ. For example, you might use an application that sends data out on port 13200, but expects the incoming response on port 13300. When you configure port triggering, you specify the trigger port range (range of outgoing ports) and the corresponding incoming range (See Figure 5.10).

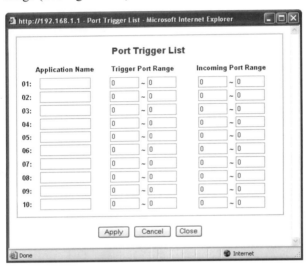

Figure 5.10: Port Triggering for Incoming and Outgoing Ports.

Check with the application's Help content or manual to determine the port trigger settings to use.

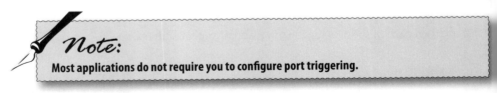

Note:

Most applications do not require you to configure port triggering.

Sharing a Broadband Connection

At this point, let's assume that your broadband connection is set up and working. Sharing the connection with the rest of the network is easy, particularly if you have a broadband router.

Sharing with a Broadband Router

Your broadband router sits between your broadband connection (DSL/Cable modem, for example) and your LAN. The router has an address on the LAN, and this is the default gateway for your network. So, enabling other computers to get on the Internet is as simple as configuring them for the proper default gateway. Open the properties for the LAN connection on the client computer and set the default gateway value to the IP address of the router (set to 192.168.0.1 in Figure 5.11). The computers should then be able to access the Internet.

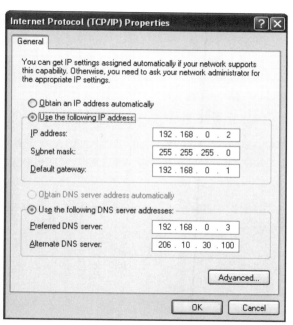

Figure 5.11: Default Gateway Setting.

What About ICS?

With the relatively low cost of today's broadband routers, I don't recommend using Internet Connection Sharing in Windows as the means for sharing a broadband connection. Using ICS requires that you install two network adapters in your computer: one for the broadband connection and another for the LAN. A decent LAN card will cost about half what a broadband router will cost, so you might as well spring for the router instead and gain the benefit of a basic firewall.

See `http://support.microsoft.com/default.aspx?scid=kb;en-us;310563` if you want more information on ICS.

Summary

It's nearly impossible these days to set up a small network without understanding TCP/IP, so this chapter offered an overview of how TCP/IP works and the role it plays in the network and routing.

Configuring a router isn't a difficult task, particularly if you're using one of the many SOHO broadband routers or access points now on the market. In most situations configuring the router is simply a matter of entering the WAN address, subnet mask, and WAN gateway supplied by your ISP, and the LAN address you've allocated for the router. You need to configure port forwarding only if you will be hosting servers on your network or need to funnel specific types of traffic to individual computers.

Sharing a broadband connection is also very easy. You simply make sure all of the computers on the LAN point to the broadband router as their default gateway. One of the easiest ways to do that is to let the router dole out that information along with IP addresses via DHCP.

For those situations where broadband isn't available but you want to share a dial-up connection, ICS in Windows can be a reasonable alternative.

Chapter 6

Securing Your Network with Firewalls

Within minutes of connecting your network to the Internet, your network is likely to be scanned for vulnerabilities, if not attacked outright. I've seen it happen more than once.

No network, whether home or small business, is complete without a firewall in place to protect it. A firewall blocks unwanted traffic and can essentially hide your network from the outside world. Even if you only connect to the Internet with a dial-up connection, you still need a firewall.

What kinds of firewalls are available? Do you need a firewall on every computer or just at the gateway? What are the configuration issues to consider when setting up a firewall? This chapter answers these questions, and more.

How Many Firewalls is Too Many?

You can implement firewalls in more than one way on the network. Each type of firewall offers certain advantages and disadvantages. Let's take a look at the possibilities.

Perimeter Only

One very workable solution is to install a firewall at the gateway and not install any local firewall software at the client computers. Often, a gateway firewall (also called a *perimeter firewall*) takes the form of a dedicated hardware device like the one shown in Figure 6.1. These dedicated firewalls sit between the Internet connection and the rest of the network.

Figure 6.1: A Typical Hardware Firewall.

A second type of firewall—a software-based firewall—is also common. This type of firewall consists of software running on a server. Two of the most popular firewalls of this type are Checkpoint FireWall-1 (www.checkpoint.com) and Microsoft Internet Security and Acceleration (ISA) Server (www.microsoft.com/isaserver).

This type of gateway firewall generally offers an excellent set of features and lots of flexibility for creating rules to fine-tune the traffic coming and going through the firewall. The other side of the coin is that the flexibility and power makes for a more complex product. That complexity translates directly to "harder to configure and manage."

If you have someone on staff who is very technically savvy, that person can probably deploy and manage one of these firewall products for you with some research and planning. If not, you should turn to a hardware-based firewall like those from Fortinet (www.fortinet.com), SonicWALL (www.sonicwall.com), D-Link (www.dlink.com),Cisco (www.cisco.com), and NETGEAR (www.netgear.com), to name a few. Each of these devices provides relatively easy configuration for someone who is technically proficient.

If your business doesn't need to host internal services or support remote access from traveling or home-based users, the firewall built into a broadband router will probably suffice. The same is true for home networks. These routers do a good job of blocking unwanted traffic, but the tradeoff for simplicity of configuration and management is a reduced set of features. It will help you block unwanted traffic, but you will have little ability to create custom rules to block or control access by specific computers on the LAN.

Tech Tip:

If you are considering putting in place a full-featured perimeter firewall, also consider whether you want to incorporate additional capabilities like antivirus scanning, spam scanning, and adware/spyware scanning. Some companies offer solutions that incorporate at least some of these additional capabilities into their firewall products.

Client Only

Another approach is to not implement a perimeter firewall but instead rely on firewall software at each computer to protect the LAN. I absolutely do not recommend this solution unless you are connecting to the Internet through a dial-up connection and therefore no place for a perimeter firewall as I described it above. However, you should implement a software firewall at the very least on the computer that serves as the dial-up connection to the Internet. You should also install and use a software-based firewall on each of the client computers on the LAN. It's particularly important that notebook computers be protected by personal firewalls, antivirus software, and spyware detection tools. Many infections on the network originate from notebooks that are used outside of the network.

Perimeter and Client

Like the concentric walls that encircled old European cities protected against the invading hordes, multiple layers of security for your network can offer better protection than a single security layer. Therefore, I recommend that you implement a combination of perimeter and client firewalls. The perimeter firewall protects the entire LAN from outside threats, and the client firewall protects the individual computer from any threats that make it past the perimeter firewall. More important, however, the client firewall can protect computers against other computers on the LAN that might become infected by Trojan horse programs or other threats.

Choosing a Perimeter Firewall

Several issues come into play when choosing a perimeter firewall, whether hardware- or software-based. This section explores these issues.

Client Licensing (Capacity)

Many firewall products are licensed (priced) based on the number of clients on the LAN they are protecting. For example, if you buy an 8-node license for your router, you can protect up to 8 computers on the LAN. The firewall tracks the number of internal addresses that connect to the Internet and blocks access by computers that exceed that number. So, your first consideration is, "How much will it cost to support the number of computers on your LAN?"

You should not try to get around the license requirements of the firewall, but there is a scenario in which the firewall won't necessarily know how many computers sit behind it. If you have some computers on a different network segment that is connected to the LAN by a device that performs NAT (such as a wireless access point), all traffic coming from that segment will hit the firewall with the same source IP address. As far as the firewall is concerned, it's all coming from the same address and therefore counts as a single IP address in the license count.

Configuration Flexibility

How you intend to use the firewall to manage traffic to and from your network is the most important factor in choosing a firewall. This section explores the common issues that fall under the broad umbrella of *configuration flexibility*—the capability to make the firewall handle the traffic in a way that suits your needs.

NAT

Chapter 5 touched on Network Address Translation (NAT). When NAT is enabled in the firewall, the firewall actively monitors all traffic coming from the LAN. The firewall inserts its own WAN address as the source IP in each outgoing packet, changes the reply port, and sends out the packet. It adds the original source IP and new reply port to the NAT table. When traffic comes in from the outside world, the firewall looks in the NAT table for an entry with a destination port that matches the one in the incoming packet. When it locates the entry, the firewall forwards the packet to the internal IP address associated with that port in the NAT table. The result is that the internal LAN is isolated from the outside world.

Firewalls offer different ways to implement NAT. The following list summarizes common options for firewall configuration:

▶ **NAT with dynamic address** — The firewall takes its WAN address dynamically from the upstream provider. This method is commonly called *overloading*.

▶ **NAT with fixed address** — The firewall has a fixed WAN address.

▶ **NAT with PPPoE** — The firewall uses Point-to-Point Protocol over Ethernet to initiate a connection to the provider's network. The provider assigns the WAN address automatically. PPPoE is not very common.

▶ **NAT disabled** — The firewall does not use NAT, but instead passes traffic unaltered.

The main factor to consider is whether the firewall you are planning to buy supports the address assignment configuration required by your provider.

Static NAT (One-to-one NAT)

Another factor to consider is whether the firewall supports one-to-one NAT assignments. With this feature, you can associate one public IP address with one internal IP address. The firewall forwards all traffic destined to the specified public address to the associated internal address. One-to-one NAT is useful when a computer on the LAN needs to be identified to the outside world by a dedicated public IP address, such as when it hosts a Web site or other service. One-to-one NAT is also useful for enabling remote access through Remote Desktop Connection and other remote access solutions without the need for port forwarding.

Some firewalls offer limited one-to-one NAT, while others enable you to associate as many public and private pairs as needed. If you need support for multiple one-to-one NAT associations, make sure the firewall you plan to buy supports it.

Port Forwarding

Even basic firewalls built into lower-end devices such as DSL routers and wireless access points generally support port forwarding. Therefore, there is little difference in port forwarding options between a higher-end firewall and a lower-end one. In all cases, you can associate a single port or a range of ports with a given internal IP address.

Port Triggering

Port triggering lets you associate a specific outgoing port with a specific incoming port. Port triggering is used by certain client-server applications and online games.

Many firewalls—but not all—support custom port triggering configuration. Here's how port triggering works: Assume you have created a port triggering entry with 2222 as the outgoing port and 3333 as the incoming port. A client on the LAN sends a packet to the firewall on port 2222. The firewall sends out the traffic on port 2222 and opens port 3333 to wait for a response. It keeps the port open for a certain period of time, and then closes it at the end of that time if not traffic is active on the port.

Unless you intend to use an application that requires port triggering, it isn't necessary that the firewall support port triggering configuration.

Custom Rules

If all you want to do is protect your LAN from typical Internet threats and don't host servers or use anything other than Web browsers and e-mail programs on the network, a simple firewall is all you need. Simple generally equals inexpensive, but it also generally equals less configuration capability.

The capability to create custom rules to manage traffic is what sets apart simple firewalls from the more capable. Almost all firewalls let you use port forwarding to manage traffic to some degree, but only the more expensive and more capable firewalls let you create custom rules that apply to specific internal IP addresses.

For example, assume that you want to allow unfettered access through the firewall to your network administrator and a handful of power users, but you want to limit another group to only using a Web browser and an e-mail client, and exclude such programs as ftp and Windows Messenger. Yet another group needs a somewhat different set of capabilities. The only way to accomplish this type of setup is to use a firewall that provides for the creation of custom, IP- or user-specific rules. Make sure the firewall you have your eye on supports this capability if you need it.

UPnP Support

If you will be using Windows Messenger or other applications that require UPnP support, make sure the firewall you choose supports UPnP. UPnP provides a mechanism for these applications to dynamically open ports in the firewall.

Using Windows XP's Firewall

Whether used in conjunction with a perimeter firewall or by itself, a client-side firewall can be a great addition to improve network security. Windows XP includes its own firewall. This section of the chapter explores the two flavors of firewall you'll find in Windows XP.

Using Internet Connection Firewall (ICF)

Versions of Windows XP prior to Service Pack 2 (SP2) include a firewall called Internet Connection Firewall, or ICF. To enable ICF, follow these steps:

1. In the Network Connections folder right-click the network connection for which you want to enable ICF.

2. Choose the **Properties** menu item, then click the **Advanced** tab (see Figure 6.2).

3. Place a check beside the option **Protect my computer and network by limiting or preventing access to this computer from the Internet**.

Figure 6.2: Advanced Tab for Network Properties.

4. To configure advanced settings for the firewall, click the **Settings** button to open the **Advanced Settings** dialog box (see Figure 6.3). The Services tab lists the services that ICF will allow in to your computer. You can click the **Add** button to open the **Service Settings** dialog box (see Figure 6.4) to add a service not listed by default. The following list summarizes the settings for a new service:

▶ **Description of service** — Enter a name for the service. The name will appear in the Services tab.

▶ **Name or IP address** — Specify the host name or IP address of the computer that hosts the service. Enter the local computer's host name if the service is hosted locally.

▶ **External Port number for this service** — Specify the port number by which computers on the Internet will access the service.

▶ **Internal Port number for this service** — Specify the internal port number on which the internal server will respond for this service.

▶ **TCP / UDP** — Choose the type of protocol used by the service.

Figure 6.3: Services Tab.

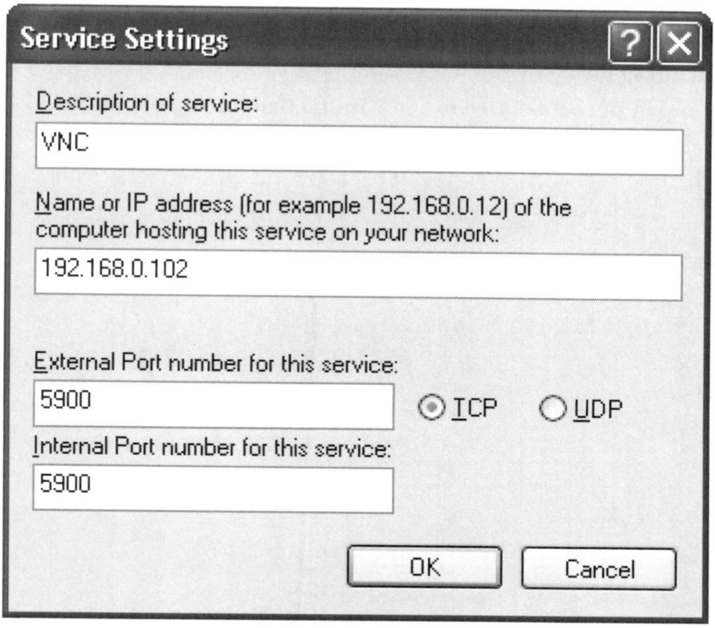

Service Settings [?][X]

Description of service:

VNC

Name or IP address (for example 192.168.0.12) of the
computer hosting this service on your network:

192.168.0.102

External Port number for this service:

5900   ⊙ TCP   ○ UDP

Internal Port number for this service:

5900

[OK]   [Cancel]

Figure 6.4: Service Settings Dialog Box.

An important point to understand about ICF is that it affects traffic that comes and goes through the network interface on which it is configured. If you are configuring ICF on a client computer, the settings you specify affect not only how computers on the Internet access resources and services on the computer, but also affect other computers on the LAN that attempt to access those services on the client computer. If you configure ICF on an interface that is part of a Internet Connection Sharing configuration, ICF affects all downstream computers on the LAN.

In a nutshell, ICF allows all outgoing traffic but blocks uninitiated incoming traffic (traffic that is not a response to an existing session). So, you can initiate an HTTP connection from your browser to a Web site, but any requests for port 80 (HTTP) that come into your computer are blocked. The same is true whether you are using ICF in a client-only configuration or as part of an ICS shared connection. As long as your local computer (client configuration) or other computer on the network (ICS configuration) hosts a service, you can just enable ICF and not create or enable any services.

Configuring Logging

The **Security Logging** tab (shown in Figure 6.5) lets you configure how ICF logs traffic. Use the **Log dropped packets** option to track traffic that the firewall drops. Use the **Log successful connections** option to log successful connections from the Internet or from other users on the LAN. You can also specify the log file location and the maximum size of the log. ICF overwrites old log entries when the maximum size is reached.

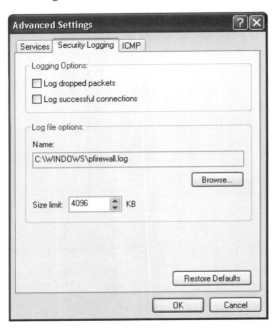

Figure 6.5: Security Logging Tab.

Configuring ICMP Handling

Internet Control Message Protocol (ICMP) enables computers to send and receive status and error information. For example, the ping command uses ICMP to send echo request packets for connection testing.

The **ICMP** tab in the **Advanced Settings** dialog box (shown in Figure 6.6) lets you control how ICF handles ICMP traffic. By default, all ICMP traffic is dropped. If you are testing a connection, you can enable **Allow incoming echo request**. When testing is complete, disable it again by clearing the check box. In most cases, I don't recommend enabling any ICMP traffic, as it is a potential source for a denial-of-service (DoS) attack.

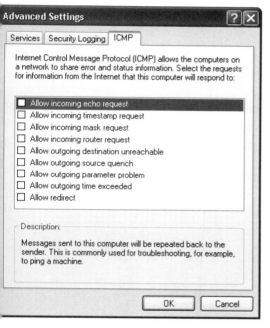

Figure 6.6: ICMP Tab.

Using Windows Firewall (Service Pack 2)

With Service Pack 2 (SP2) for Windows XP, Microsoft introduced several changes to the integrated Windows firewall and renamed the service Windows Firewall. You'll find several cosmetic differences in Windows Firewall from ICF, but Windows Firewall also incorporates several functional differences:

▶ **Common configuration** — When you configure Windows Firewall, all network interfaces are configured with the specified settings, making it easy to protect all network and dial-up connections with the same group of settings. You can, however, make individual changes to each interface.

▶ **Scope** — Windows Firewall enables you to specify the *scope* for a rule. Scope determines the source addresses to which the rule applies. Available scopes include:

  • **Global** — This scope applies to all source addresses, whether on the Internet or the LAN.

- **Subnet** — This scope applies to all source addresses within a specified subnet.

- **Custom list** — Use this scope to create a custom list of individual addresses and subnets to which the rule applies.

▶ **Exceptions** — You can specify exceptions on a per-application basis. Exceptions allow the excepted program to work through the firewall.

▶ **On by default** — Windows Firewall is enabled by default when you install SP2. You can disable Windows Firewall manually (Windows prompts you at the first startup after SP2 installation), or use group policy to configure the firewall.

▶ **Boot time security** — Unlike ICF, Windows Firewall provides protection for the computer as it is booting and before the Windows interface is loaded. Windows Firewall allows a very minimal set of services access to the computer to support DHCP and a handful of other boot traffic requirements.

▶ **On with no exceptions** — You can enable this mode with a single click to lock down the computer and disallow all unrequested traffic.

▶ **Full group policy support** — Windows Firewall fully supports configuration with group policy for Windows Server Active Directory domains and local policy.

▶ **Support for RPC** — Windows Firewall handles Remote Procedure Call (RPC) traffic differently from ICF. Any RPC server application that is running in the Local System, Network Service, or Local Service security context can request that Windows Firewall open the necessary ports to enable the service to handle incoming requests. You can also add an RPC application to the exceptions list to enable the application to accept incoming traffic on dynamically-assigned ports.

▶ **Multicast responses** — Windows Firewall allows a unicast response for three seconds on the same port from which a multicast or broadcast packet arrived, enabling applications and services to alter firewall policy for multicast and broadcast client/server situations.

▶ **IPv4 and IPv6 support** — Windows Firewall supports both the IPv4 and IPv6 protocols with a single firewall and interface, eliminating the need to configure two firewalls on systems that use IPv6.

Configuring Windows Firewall

To configure Windows Firewall, open the **Windows Firewall** applet from the Control Panel. The **General** tab lets you enable or disable the firewall, and enable the **Don't allow exceptions** mode.

The **Exceptions** tab is the place to go to add, modify, or delete exceptions for specific programs. Windows defines a small number of exceptions by default, and it also can add exceptions automatically as programs attempt to access Internet resources.

Windows Firewall provides two ways to add exceptions. First, Windows Firewall will prompt you when an application attempts to establish a connection that requires opening an incoming port. If you direct the firewall to allow the application, Windows Firewall adds the application to the Exceptions list.

You can also add applications or ports manually. Add a program exception when you want to allow a specific program to receive incoming data through the firewall. To add a program, click **Add Program** to display the **Add a Program** dialog box. Select the program from the supplied list or browse for the program's main executable file. By default, Windows Firewall configures the exception for global scope, but you can click the **Change Scope** button to reduce the scope of the rule.

You can also add a port exception. Creating a port exception allows all incoming traffic on the specified port, essentially opening a hole in the firewall for that port only. All applications will be able to receive through the incoming port. To add a port exception, click the **Add Port** button on the **Exceptions** tab to open the **Add a Port** dialog box (see Figure 6.7). Enter a name for the exception and enter the port number. Click the **Change Scope** button if you need to reduce the rule's scope (the default scope is global), then click the **OK** button on the **Add a Port** dialog box to create the exception.

Add a Port

Use these settings to open a port through Windows Firewall. To find the port number and protocol, consult the documentation for the program or service you want to use.

Name: VNC

Port number: 5900

◉ TCP   ○ UDP

What are the risks of opening a port?

[Change scope...]   [OK]   [Cancel]

Figure 6.7: Add a Port Dialog Box.

The **Advanced** tab (shown in Figure 6.8) is the place to go to enable or disable the firewall for a specific interface and change the firewall settings for an interface. You can also configure logging and ICMP properties, which were discussed in the previous section on ICF.

Windows Firewall

| General | Exceptions | Advanced |

Network Connection Settings

Windows Firewall is enabled for the connections selected below. To add exceptions for an individual connection, select it, and then click Settings:

☑ 1394 Connection
☑ 3Sharp
☑ Local Area Connection
☑ Rothsay

[Settings...]

Security Logging

You can create a log file for troubleshooting purposes.   [Settings...]

ICMP

With Internet Control Message Protocol (ICMP), the computers on a network can share error and status information.   [Settings...]

Default Settings

To restore all Windows Firewall settings to a default state, click Restore Defaults.   [Restore Defaults]

[OK]   [Cancel]

Figure 6.8: Advanced Tab.

To enable or disable the firewall for a particular interface, check or uncheck the interface in the **Network Connection Settings** group. To set properties for a specific interface, click the interface in the list and then click the **Settings** button. Windows Firewall opens the **Services** tab, where you can enable, add, and remove service entries for the interface. For more details on working with services, see the section "Using Internet Connection Firewall," earlier in this chapter. For a complete discussion of Windows Firewall, see *Microsoft Windows XP Power Productivity*, Sybex, 2005.

Using Third-Party Firewall Programs

ICF and Windows Firewall have the advantage of being free and included with Windows. The changes introduced with Windows Firewall in SP2 make it a viable option for users who need a client-side firewall solution. However, even with its improvements, Windows Firewall doesn't offer all of the features you'll find in some of the third-party client firewall programs.

These are some of the more popular third-party firewall programs:

▶ **ZoneAlarm** — See `www.zonelabs.com`.

▶ **BlackICE PC Protection** — See `www.blackice.com`.

▶ **Tiny Firewall** — See `www.tinysoftware.com`.

Each of these programs offers an excellent set of features and incorporates additional features outside of the basic firewall functions to further improve performance. For example, Tiny Personal Firewall actively monitors system resources such as the Registry and critical Windows systems files to prevent changes and help avoid virus and spyware infections.

Summary

No network is safe without a firewall of some kind. In every case for a small office network, I recommend a perimeter firewall to block unwanted traffic before it gets to the network. The addition of client-side firewalls such as Windows Firewall, ZoneAlarm, or Tiny Firewall add an extra layer of protection against threats from the LAN as well as the outside world. For home networks, the firewall built into a broadband router can serve as an adequate first line of defense against network-borne threats. In a small network with a shared dial-up connection, Windows Firewall or ICF on the gateway computer is a good solution, but should be supplemented by client-side firewalls.

If the LAN will host servers for Web, mail, or other purposes, you must configure port forwarding in the firewall to pass the traffic to the server(s). In networks with more than one server for a given port, the firewall must support one-to-one NAT, enabling you to associate a separate public IP address with each internal server.

Finally, you also need to consider client access issues for router configuration. Determine what applications require incoming ports to be opened and configure port forwarding and port triggering accordingly.

Chapter 7

Setting Up Network Clients

After you have set up the network infrastructure and installed and configured devices such as the router and firewall, it's time to set up the network clients. This phase of the network setup process involves installing networking hardware in each computer, configuring the network protocol settings, and testing access.

This chapter focuses on network hardware installation and configuration. By the end of this chapter, your network should be up and running with all of your wired computers accessing the network. For wireless configuration, see Chapter 9.

Installing Wired Network Adapters

Each client computer that will connect to the LAN needs some type of network interface hardware. The installation process varies somewhat depending on the operating system being used, but the process is similar. The first step is to install the hardware.

> **Note:**
> If you are using a USB network adapter, you only need to plug the adapter into one of the computer's USB ports. Read the documentation to determine if you need to install software on the computer prior to plugging in the USB adapter. Many USB devices do not require additional software when installed on Windows XP, but most USB devices installed on earlier operating systems do require additional software.

Installing the Hardware

Before you rush out to buy network adapters for all of your computers, first determin
whether any of the computers includes a built-in network interface. Most newer computer
include a network interface integrated onto the motherboard, eliminating the need t
install additional hardware.

Tech Tip:
Read the network adapter's documentation before installing the device. In most cases you do not
have to install any software or drivers prior to installing the card, but verify that beforehand.

If you do need to install network adapters, you should follow these general guidelines t
avoid damage to the card or the computer:

► **Turn it off** — You can't install or remove adapters from the computer when
it is on. To avoid damage to the computer or personal injury, make sure the
computer is turned off while you work on it.

► **Provide adequate grounding** — The other devices in the computer
and the network card are susceptible to damage from static electricity.
You should discharge any static prior to touching the card or other items
inside the computer. Do so by touching a grounded metal object, such as
the computer's internal case. Avoid working on carpet. You can also use
a grounding strap that attaches to your wrist and to a grounded object to
prevent additional static build-up.

► **Handle the card as little as possible** — In addition to discharging any
static before handling the card, limit the amount of time you touch the card.
Whenever possible, avoid touching chips on the card or the contacts. Handle
the card by the bracket, if possible.

► **Seat and secure the card properly** — When inserting the card into its slot,
press straight down on the card. Make sure the card is fully seated in its
socket, then secure the card with a screw (unless the chassis uses a different
method to secure the adapter cards).

What happens after you install the card depends on the operating system you are using. Windows XP will generally find most cards at startup and if Windows has a driver for the card, installs the driver automatically. If Windows does not have a driver for the card, you must install the driver yourself.

Regardless of the version of Windows you are running, Windows should identify the adapter at startup and start a wizard to prompt you through the driver installation. Check the documentation that comes with the card to determine how to install the drivers for your version of Windows.

Configuring the Card

In many situations, you do not need to configure settings for the network interface for it to work properly. Sometimes, however, some adjustments are required. For example, you might want to configure the adapter for 100Mbps rather than autosense to ensure that the adapter always comes up in 100Mbps mode rather than 10Mbps.

Windows 98 and Windows Me

To manage adapter settings on a Windows 98 or Me computer, first open the Device Manager. Right-click **Network Neighborhood** and choose the **Properties** menu item (see Figure 7.1).

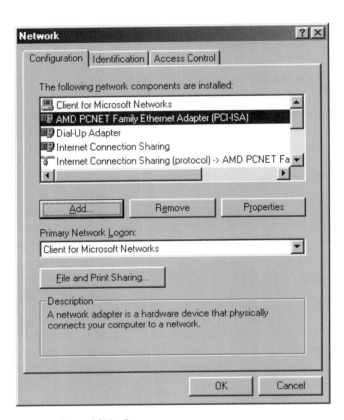

Figure 7.1: Network Dialog Box.

To configure adapter properties, select the adapter in the list and click the **Properties** button to display the property dialog box shown in Figure 7.2.

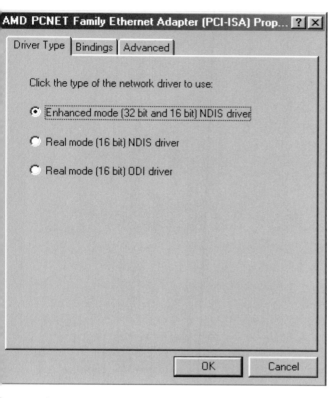

Figure 7.2: Driver Type Tab.

The **Driver Type** tab lets you specify the type of network driver to use. Unless the network adapter requires a real-mode driver that must be loaded through `autoexec.bat` or `config.sys`, use the **Enhanced mode** option (which loads the driver within Windows).

The **Bindings** tab (shown in Figure 7.3) lets you specify which protocols are bound to the adapter. If a protocol is not bound, the protocol is not available through that interface.

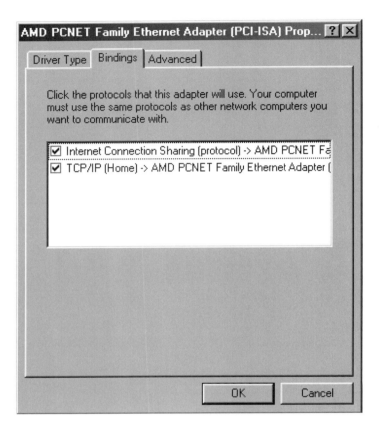

Figure 7.3: Bindings Tab.

In most situations, you will not need to configure the majority (if any) of the setting
for a network adapter. When you do need to configure a setting, the **Advanced** tab (see
Figure 7.4) lets you configure adapter-specific settings, such as speed, duplex, and more
Specify settings as needed and click the OK button, then click the OK button to close the
properties for the network connection. Windows 98/Me systems require a restart for the
change to take effect.

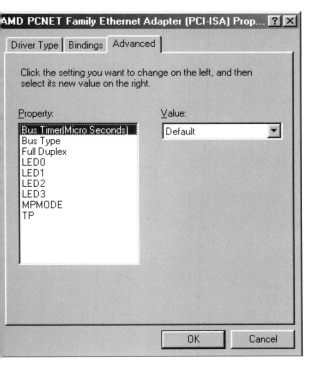

igure 7.4: Advanced Tab.

Windows 2000, XP, and 2003

n Windows 2000, open the Network and Dial-up Connections folder, right-click the network connection, and choose the **Properties** menu item. In Windows XP/2003, open he Network Connections folder, right-click the connection and choose the **Properties** menu item to open the dialog box shown in Figure 7.5. Then, click the **Configure** button o open the device's property dialog box.

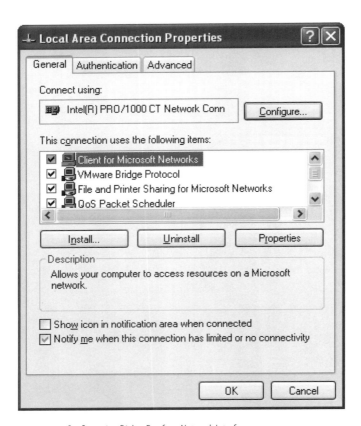

Figure 7.5: Configuration Dialog Box for a Network Interface.

The **General** tab of the device's properties provides some basic information about the device, such as manufacturer. You can use the **Driver** tab to view details about the driver, such as provider, date, and version. You can also update the driver from this tab.

The **Advanced** tab (see Figure 7.6) lets you specify adapter-specific properties such as speed, duplex mode, network address, and so on. The settings available on the **Advance** tab vary by adapter model. Set a particular setting only if you have a specific need to do so. In most cases, the default settings will work without modification.

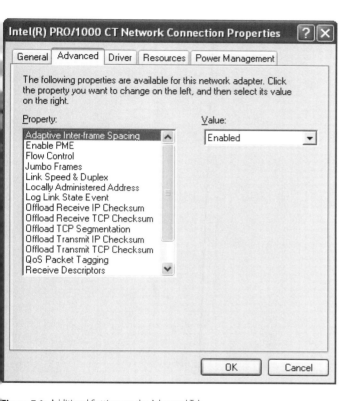

Figure 7.6: Additional Settings on the Advanced Tab.

Most of today's devices support Plug-and-Play (PnP) configuration, which enables the computer and operating system to automatically configure devices to prevent resource conflicts. In situations where the device does not support PnP or you must manually configure resource settings, turn to the **Resources** tab for the device (shown in Figure 7.7). You can also use the **Resources** tab to view current settings for PnP-configured devices.

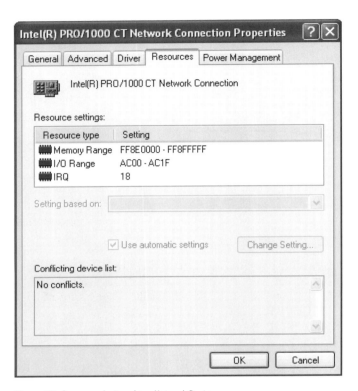

Figure 7.7: Resources Assigned to a Network Device.

Tech Tip:
You can view resource assignments for all devices in the Device Manager. Choose the View⇨ Resources by Type menu item.

Making the Connections

After installing the network interface, you naturally need to connect the computer to the network. If you followed the advice in Chapter 4, you installed a modular drop or other type of RJ45 receptacle near each computer. Connecting the computer to the network is as simple as plugging in a manufactured patch cable into the computer and the receptacle.

After you connect the computer to the network, boot the computer and check for a link light on the network card, if it includes a link light. If not, check for a link light at the switch or hub. The link light will not be lit until the network interface is initialized, so it can take several seconds before you see a light. If there is no link light, even after the computer has fully started, check the connections and try a different patch cable. If there is still no link light, verify with a cable tester or working computer that the network connection works. If not, check the connections at the switch. If there is still no connectivity, you probably have a bad cable run.

Choosing a Network Client

When you install the network adapter, Windows automatically adds a network protocol and network client. This section explains network client selection and installation.

Windows 98

All versions from Windows 98SE and on install TCP/IP by default, along with the Client for Microsoft Networks. The client provides logon capability and related services.

Windows 98 offers six network clients:

► **Banyan DOS/Windows 3.1 client** — This client offers connectivity for Banyan networks. It is not likely that you will require this client in a SOHO network.

► **Client for Microsoft Networks** — This is the default client for Microsoft-based networks and the one I recommend for your network. This client displays the **Enter Network Password** dialog box (see Figure 7.8) at startup.

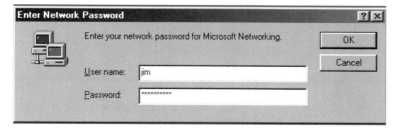

Figure 7.8: Authentication Dialog Box for Client for Microsoft Networks.

► **Client for NetWare Networks** — This Microsoft client provides logon and related services for NetWare networks.

► **Microsoft Family Logon** — This client provides simplified logon, as shown in Figure 7.9. However, I have experienced many problems over the years with this client and therefore don't recommend its use.

Figure 7.9: Microsoft Family Logon Authentication Dialog Box.

► **Novell NetWare 3.x** — This Novell-provided client provides logon and related services for NetWare 3.x networks.

► **Novell NetWare 4.x** — This Novell-provided client provides logon and related services for NetWare 4.x and later networks.

Follow these steps to add one of the clients included with Windows:

1. Right-click **Network Neighborhood** and choose the **Properties** menu item.

2. In the **Configuration** tab, click the **Add** button.

3. Choose **Client** from the network component list and click the **Add** button.

4. Select the client manufacturer from the **Manufacturers** list (see Figure 7.10) and then select the client from the **Network Clients** list. Click the **OK** button to continue.

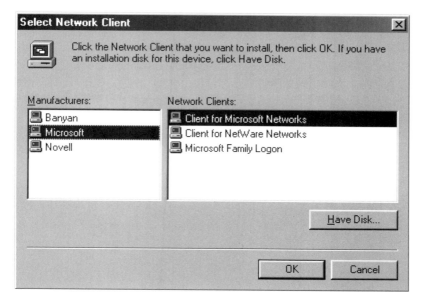

Figure 7.10: Select Network Client Dialog Box.

5. Windows will prompt you for the Windows CD or path to the Windows source files on the computer's hard disk. Follow the prompts to complete the installation. You must restart the computer to make the change take effect.

Tech Tip:
In addition to these clients that are included with Windows, you can also add other network clients provided by a network vendor. Click the Have Disk button in Step 4 to choose the client from the vendor-provided diskette, CD, or download location.

Windows 2000, Windows XP, and Windows 2003

Windows 2000, Windows XP, and Windows 2003 all include and install the Client for Microsoft Networks by default. These three operating systems also offer one additional client, the Client Service for NetWare, which offers logon and related services for NetWare networks.

Follow these steps if you need to add a network client in one of these operating systems:

1. Open the Network Connections folder from the Control Panel, right-click the network interface, and choose the **Properties** menu item.

2. Click the **Install** button in the **General** tab to open the **Select Network Component Type** dialog box.

3. Click the **Add** button to open the **Select Network Client** dialog box (see Figure 7.11), select the client, and click the **OK** button.

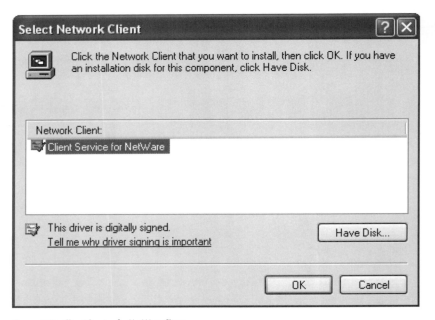

Figure 7.11: Client Service for NetWare Client.

4. Follow the Windows prompts to complete the installation.

Adding Protocols

From Windows 98 on, Windows installs the TCP/IP protocol automatically when you add a network adapter to the computer, and configures TCP/IP for dynamic addressing through DHCP.

You can add other protocols to a computer to suit your networking requirements. For example, you might add the AppleTalk protocol in networks where older Macs and Mac-based printers are present.

Follow these steps in Windows 98/Me to add a protocol:

1. Open the properties for the network connection and, from the **Configuration** tab, click the **Add** button.

2. In the **Select Network Component Type** dialog box, choose **Protocol** and click the **Add** button.

3. In the **Select Network Protocol** dialog box (see Figure 7.12), choose the manufacturer in the left pane and the protocol in the right pane, and then click the **OK** button.

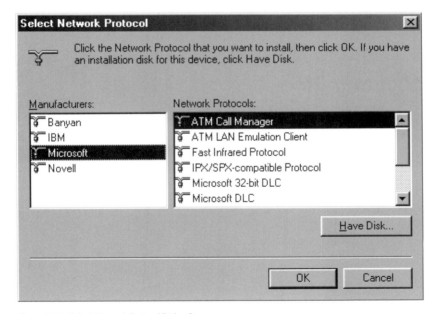

Figure 7.12: Select Network Protocol Dialog Box.

4. Follow the Windows prompts to complete the installation.

Note:
Some protocols require additional configuration. After installing the protocol, click the protocol in the **Network** dialog box and click the **Properties** button.

Follow these steps in Windows 2000 and later to add a protocol:

1. Open the properties for the network interface and, in the **General** tab, click the **Install** button.

2. Choose **Protocol** from the **Select Network Component Type** dialog box and click the **Add** button.

3. Choose the protocol from the **Network Protocols** list and click the **OK** button.

4. Follow the Windows prompts to complete the installation.

Configuring Other Network Settings

When you have finished setting up clients and protocols, it's time to turn your attention to a handful of other network-related settings. The following sections explain these settings for various operating systems.

Windows 98

Each computer has a unique presence on the network. In part, this presence is dictated by the computer's IP address (assuming TCP/IP is installed). In addition, the computer's name is also used to identify it on the network. As Chapter 8 explains, for example, you can map to a shared network folder using the sharing computer's name. The computer name must be unique on the network.

The computer can also belong to a *workgroup*. The workgroup helps organize computers in the network and simplifies browsing for network resources such as shared folders and printers. Workgroups do not provide any security or segregation of resources. When you browse the network, you see the computers in the same workgroup by default. However, you can browse and connect to resources in other workgroups, subject to the permissions of the account you use to access those resources. The default workgroup name in Windows 98 is workgroup.

Tech Tip:

Putting a computer in a different workgroup is as easy as changing the workgroup name in the network connection's properties, as explained later in this section.

To set a computer's name or workgroup in Windows 98, follow these steps:

1. Right-click **Network Neighborhood** and choose the **Properties** menu item.

2. Click the **Identification** tab (see Figure 7.13). The **Computer Name** field on the **Identification** tab lists the computer's name.

3. Type a new, unique name for the computer in this field. To change the computer's workgroup, enter the desired workgroup name in the **Workgroup** field.

4. Click the **OK** button and restart the computer to make the changes take effect.

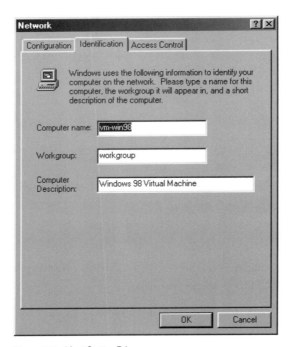

Figure 7.13: Identification Tab.

Note:

Microsoft offers a directory services client to enable Windows 98 computers to have limited participation in Active Directory. See http://www.microsoft. com/windows2000/server/evaluation/news/bulletins/adextension. asp **for details.**

Windows 2000

Windows 2000 computers can participate in a workgroup or be configured as domain members participating in an Active Directory domain. As with Windows 98, you can also change the name assigned to a computer.

To change the computer's name, right-click **My Computer** and choose the **Properties** menu item (or open the **System** applet from the Control Panel). Then, click the **Network Identification** tab (as shown in Figure 7.14).

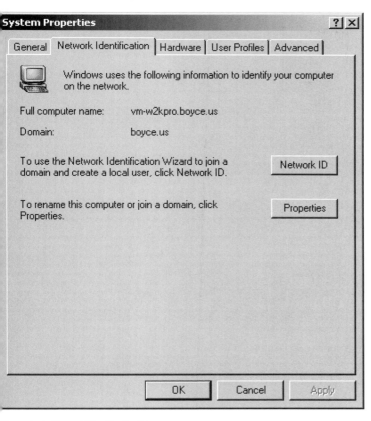

Figure 7.14: Network Identification Tab.

The **Network Identification** tab lists the computer's current name and workgroup or domain name. To change the computer name or workgroup/domain membership, click the **Properties** button to open the **Identification Changes** dialog box (see Figure 7.15). Use the **Computer Name** field to change the computer name and the **Member Of** group to specify the workgroup name or make the computer a domain member.

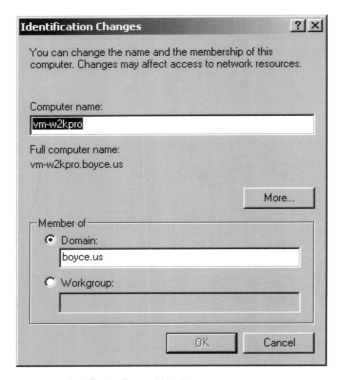

Figure 7.15: Identification Changes Dialog Box.

Note:
To add a computer to a domain, you must specify a domain account that has the permissions, either directly or through group membership, required to add computers to the domain.

Windows XP and Windows 2003

The process for changing computer name, workgroup, or domain is very similar in Windows XP and Windows 2003 to Windows 2000. The main difference is the interface.

Open the **System** applet from the Control Panel or right-click **My Computer** and choose the **Properties** menu item. Click the **Computer Name** tab (shown in Figure 7.16). Use the **Computer description** field to add an optional description for the computer that will appear beside the computer name when users browse the network for resources.

Figure 7.16: Computer Name Tab.

Next, click the **Change** button to display the **Computer Name Changes** dialog box. Enter the new computer name in the Computer name field, and use the **Domain** or **Workgroup** options to specify the workgroup or domain membership. As with Windows 2000, you must specify an account that has the necessary permissions to add computers to a domain if changing domains or changing from a workgroup to a domain.

Summary

When installing network hardware or performing any other work inside a computer, take care to avoid damaging the computer or the network card with static electricity. Always ground yourself prior to touching the card or other devices inside the computer. Obviously, always make sure the computer is off before you open it.

In the majority of SOHO networks, the default network settings, clients, and protocols will suffice to enable computers to share resources and access the Internet (if available). In rare situations, you might need to add an additional protocol or client. You do so through the properties for the network connection.

Finally, keep in mind that you can change the computer's network name and membership in a workgroup or Active Directory domain. You accomplish these changes through the **System** applet in the Control Panel.

Using and
Extending the
Network

Chapter 8

Sharing and Securing Network Resources

Most people want to do more with their network than just share an Internet connection. Some want to share folders and printers, others want to play games across the network, and still others have more advanced needs, such as adding a server to enable such tasks as application and database sharing.

This chapter focuses on sharing folders and printers, the two most common reasons for implementing a SOHO network. Sharing folders will enable you to not only share documents, but also share downloaded music, digital photos, and more.

First, let's take a look at server-based sharing, a common use for small business networks.

Server-Based Sharing

One scenario for sharing folders and printers is to set up a dedicated server to host the shared resources. The best choice for the server operating system depends on several factors. Linux is a reasonable choice when you have someone on staff who can dedicate the time to learning and managing the server. This usually isn't the case in a small network. Therefore, following sections offer recommendations for choosing between Windows Server and Windows XP Professional.

> **Note:**
> If you are setting up sharing for a home network, skip to the section "Peer-to-Peer Sharing," later in this chapter.

Number of Concurrent Users and Licensing

Windows XP Professional supports up to ten concurrent connections, which will accommodate up to ten users on the network at a time. The network can contain any number of client workstations, but only ten can access resources at the same time.

Windows Server supports an unlimited number of connections, subject to the number of CALs you purchase.

When you buy Windows Server, you receive a server license that allows you to install the operating system on one computer. A server license by itself doesn't give you the legal right to allow others to connect to that computer, whether they work for your company or not. Instead, each user needs a Client Access License, or CAL. You might think that buying a copy of Windows XP or other Windows operating system gives you that CAL but it doesn't. When you buy a Windows client operating system you have the legal right to install it on a computer and use it, but the Windows license does not give you the legal right to use it to connect to a Windows Server. That's where the CALs come in.

A CAL gives you the legal right to connect to a server application such as Windows Server. Not all CALs are created equal, however. A CAL is targeted to a specific server application.

For example, in order for ten users to connect to a Windows Server to access shared printers and folders, you need to purchase ten Windows CALs. Windows Server keeps track of the connections by computer, so multiple concurrent connections from one computer count only against one license. For example, you could open four shared folders and use two shared printers concurrently, and this would count as one connection rather than six.

Now, let's throw Exchange Server into the mix. If you have 25 users, you need to purchase 25 Exchange Server CALs in addition to 25 Windows CALs for that server. Likewise other Microsoft server applications such as SQL Server, Project Server, Host Integration Server, and others, require their own CALs. Let's expand the example and say that you have 25 users who need access to the server for printing and file sharing. 20 of those users need access to Exchange Server, and 10 need access to SQL Server. You need 25 Windows CALs, 20 Exchange Server CALs, and 10 SQL Server CALs, for a total of 55 CALs.

Sounds simple enough, doesn't it? In an example like this it is simple, but what if several of your Exchange Server users need to access the server from a desktop computer, a notebook, and a PDA? What if you add a shop floor where 50 employees share 10 computers in different shifts? Now you need to consider licensing modes.

Note:

Microsoft does not require a Client Access License (CAL) for users to access a Windows XP-based server.

Choose Your Mode

Windows 2000 Server offers two licensing modes: per-server and per-seat. Windows Server 2003 replaces per-seat licensing with per-user/per-device. Let's take per-server first.

When you configure Windows Server for per-server mode, you specify the number of CALs you have purchased for the server and Windows Server allows up to that number of concurrent connections. Configure it for 100 CALs, for example, and Windows Server will support up to 100 concurrent connections. Additional connection attempts after the limit is reached will fail. Windows Server counts administrator connections against the total but still allows administrators to connect after the limit is reached to allow them to manage the server (and potentially disconnect users if needed). Therefore, with per-server licensing, Windows Server actively controls connections based on the number of licenses for which you have configured it.

Per-user/per-seat mode is a bit different. A User CAL (per-user mode) allows a single user to connect to the server with any number of devices. If your users work with a desktop computer, notebook, PDA, and smart phone—all accessing an Exchange Server, for example—the logical choice would be to purchase User CALs. Each user could then connect with as many devices as needed.

A Device CAL allows one device to connect to the server application. For example, assume you have a training lab containing 20 computers that are shared by 200 students throughout the day. Rather than purchase 200 User CALs, you would instead purchase 20 Device CALs. Since User CALs and Device CALs cost the same, your licensing cost is only one-tenth what it would be if you purchased User CALs.

An important distinction between per-server and per-user/per-device licensing is that with the latter, Windows Server does not prevent connections even after the limit is reached. The License Logging service does monitor and report connections for both per-server and per-user/per-device, but only with per-server mode does Windows deny connections after the limit is reached.

I Don't Need No Stinking CAL!

There are a few situations where CALs are not needed. The first is when users access the server anonymously. For example, you don't need CALs to allow users to access your company's Web site. If you add a private area to the site that requires authentication, such as to allow access to key customers or business partners, you do need to add CALs for those users who will be authenticating.

Recognizing that companies might require a large number of customers or clients to access a server or server application, Microsoft introduced the External Connector License. An External Connector (EC) allows an unlimited number of external users to access a particular server application. ECs are not meant to allow company employees to connect remotely—you need traditional CALs for that. Instead, ECs are targeted at customers, clients, and business partners who need authenticated access to your servers and server applications.

ECs can be expensive if you don't have very many customers or partners at the moment who need access. If that's the case, you can purchase CALs and achieve the same legal goal. If the number of external users will grow over time, compare the cost of individual CALs against the cost of an EC to determine which option makes the most sense for your situation.

For more information about CALs and licensing, check out Microsoft's CAL Guide at its Software Asset Management site, http://www.microsoft.com/resources/sam/lic_cal.mspx.

Additional Services

Windows Server includes many additional services that you might need on a small network. The most common include the following:

▶ **DHCP** — The DHCP service enables a Windows Server to allocate DHCP address leases (see Figure 8.1). In most small networks, the broadband router or firewall can also perform the same function.

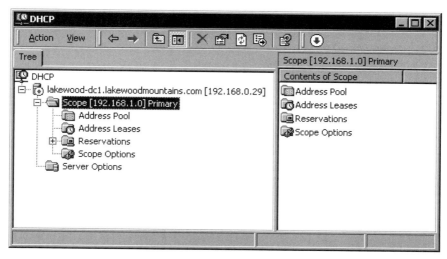

Figure 8.1: DHCP Administrative Console.

► **DNS** — The DNS service provides name-to-address resolution for Web browsing, e-mail, and other services. In almost every case, your upstream service provider will provide DNS services for you.

► **Active Directory** — The Active Directory (see Figure 8.2) provides simplified authentication for resources located on servers and workstations across the network. The AD also can simplify resource access by enabling an administrator to publish resources. The AD is a requirement of many server applications such as Exchange Server.

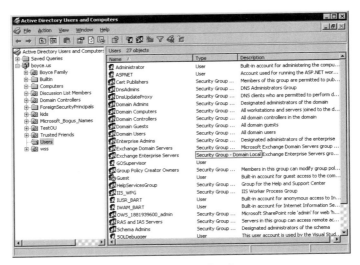

Figure 8.2: Active Directory Users and Computers Console.

▶ **Internet Information Services** — IIS provides the capability to host Web and FTP sites, along with related services (see Figure 8.3). Windows Server 2003 includes Windows SharePoint Services, which provides a means for users to easily share documents and other information.

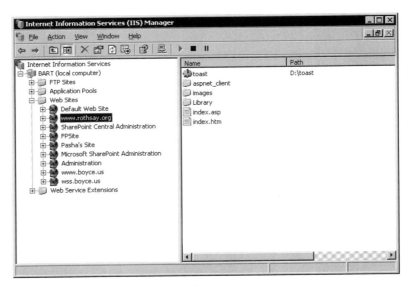

Figure 8.3: Internet Information Services Console.

▶ **Terminal Server** — This service enables users to run remote sessions on the server to access shared applications. Each user or device requires a Terminal Server CAL.

▶ **Routing and Remote Access (RRAS)** — This provides for routing, remote dial-up access, and remote VPN access to the network. If some of your users need secure remote access to the LAN from home or other locations, RRAS can provide this capability. However, it's possible that your firewall can also provide VPN access.

▶ **File Services for Macintosh (FSM)** — Use this service to integrate Macs and PCs on the network. FSM enables Macintosh users to access shared folders on the server, allowing Mac and PC users to easily share files.

Cost and Administrative Overhead

Windows Server is roughly four times the cost of Windows XP Professional (currently just over $1,000 with ten CALs). Additional CALs are relatively inexpensive. Therefore, Windows Server 2003 Standard Edition is a good solution for small businesses that need to support more than ten concurrent users or that need the additional services and performance offered by Windows Server.

Because Windows Server provides an interface that is very similar to Windows XP, most people with a good computer background and technical understanding can install and manage a server in a small network without extra training or an IT degree. As the number of users and services hosted increases, the more complex the network and server become, potentially requiring someone with specific training and the time to devote to server management.

If you have less than ten users and only need to share folders and a printer or two, Windows XP Professional is a low-cost alternative to Windows Server that will offer good results.

Peer-to-Peer Sharing

In a peer-to-peer network, most devices on the network act as peers, sharing some of their resources with the network. For example, you might share a folder on each user's computer to enable others to access certain documents. In a peer-based network, computers can also share their printers with others on the LAN. Users can browse the workgroup to locate resources on each computer, as shown in Figure 8.4.

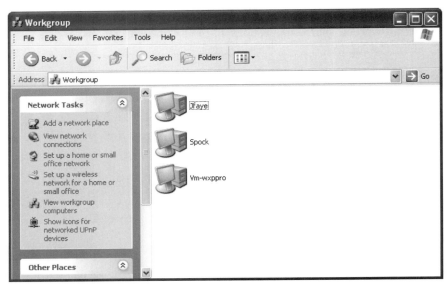

Figure 8.4: Browsing a Workgroup for Computers.

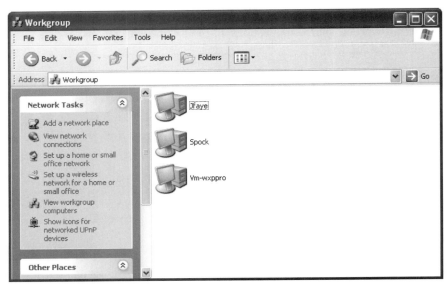 *Note:*

All versions of Windows in use today provide peer sharing. This section focuses on Windows XP.

While peer-sharing is easy to set up and manage, it comes with one drawback—the lack of centralized authentication and administration. In a server-based network, users specify a user name and password to connect to shared resources. If the user's local logon account also exists on the server and the passwords are the same, access is transparent to the user—he doesn't have to specify any account credentials to access a folder or printer, for example. This is true whether the server is running Windows Server or Windows XP.

However, if a user needs to access resources on more than one peer computer on the LAN, he must have an account on each of those computers. As with a server-based scenario, Windows authenticates automatically if the local user credentials match those on the remote computer. If not, the user must specify the user name and password for the shared resources on the remote computer.

As the number of computers sharing resources on the LAN goes up, so does the complexity of managing all those accounts. Therefore, peer sharing is useful in very small networks (such as at home) and less so as the network grows. In most situations, a single, centralized server (regardless of its operating system) makes the most sense.

See the section "Backup Considerations" later in this chapter for more reasons to consider single server designs.

Configuring Accounts and Permissions

Whether you are using server- or peer-based sharing, one of the first steps is to create and configure the accounts that people will use to access shared resources.

Creating Accounts in Windows Server

If you are not using Active Directory, you create accounts on Windows Server in the same way as on Windows XP. See the following section, "Creating Accounts in Windows XP," for details.

When Active Directory is used, you rely on the **Active Directory Users and Computers** console to create accounts:

1. Open the **Active Directory Users and Computers** console from the Administrative Tools folder.

2. In the left pane (see Figure 8.5), click the Organizational Unit (OU) where you want the account to reside. In most small networks, you can simply place new users in the Users container. If you instead want to create a separate OU, right-click the domain and choose the **New⇨ Organizational Unit** menu item. Then, type an OU name and click the **OK** button.

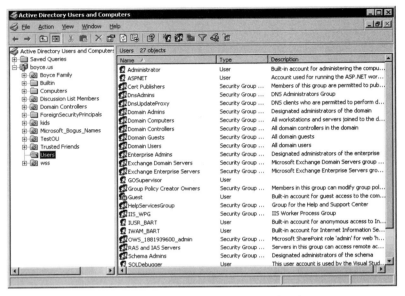

Figure 8.5: Users Branch in the Active Directory Users and Computers Console.

3. After you select the target container, choose the **Action**⇨ **New**⇨ **User** menu item, or simply click the **New User** button on the toolbar to open the **New Object - User** dialog box.

4. Enter the user's name in the **First name** and **Last name** fields, and then enter a logon account name in the **User logon name** field. Click the **Next** button.

5. Enter a password and confirm it in the **Password** and **Confirm password** fields.

6. Configure the remaining options using the following list as a guide:

    ▶ **User must change password at next logon** — Choose this option to force the user to change password the next time he logs on.

    ▶ **User cannot change password** — Choose this option to prevent the user from changing his password.

    ▶ **Password never expires** — Choose this option if you don't want Windows Server to prompt the user to change password when the password age limit is reached.

▶ **Account is disabled** — Choose this option to disable the account. Right-click an account and choose the **Enable Account** menu item to re-enable a disabled account.

7. Click the **Next** button then click the **Finish** button.

Tech Tip:

You can add users to groups to further organize security and resource access. For a complete description of groups and the Active Directory, see, *Windows Server 2003 Bible* from Wiley.

Creating Accounts in Windows XP

Windows XP does not include Active Directory, so all accounts are local accounts. Follow these steps to create accounts on a Windows XP Professional computer:

1. Right-click My Computer and choose the **Manage** menu item to open the **Computer Management** console (see Figure 8.6).

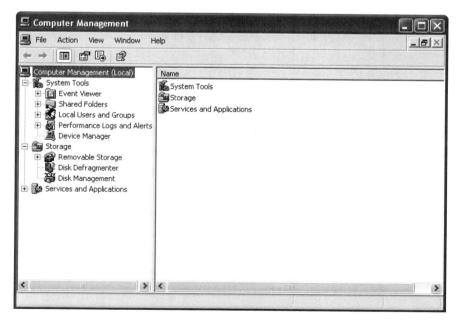

Figure 8.6: Computer Management Console.

2. Expand the **Local Users and Groups** branch, right-click **Users**, and choose the **New User** menu item to open the **New User** dialog box.

3. Enter the logon account name in the **User name** field and the user's name in the **Full name** field.

4. Enter and confirm the password in the **Password** and **Confirm Password** fields.

5. Set other options as desired (see the previous section for details) and click the **Create** button. P154

Sharing Folders and Files

After you set up accounts, you're ready to start sharing folders. This section explains how to do so, and the issues to consider.

Caution:

You should always protect a private network from a public one such as the Internet with a firewall. Never share folders on an unprotected network or computers with public IP addresses.

Choosing the File System

The first issue to consider is the file system to be used by the computer that is sharing its resources. You have two options on a Windows computer:

▶ **FAT** — The FAT file system, which includes several versions up to FAT32, is the easiest type of file system to manage. However, FAT offers no folder- or file-level security. Anyone with a local account can access folders in a FAT volume. FAT volumes are limited to the share permissions Change, Read, and Full Control. FAT is available on all Windows versions.

▶ **NTFS** — This file system is available on Windows NT, Windows 2000, Windows XP, and Windows Server. NTFS offers good folder- and file-level security, enabling you to control access to specific files by specific users. NTFS is the best choice for securing folders and files but requires a bit more knowledge and effort to configure permissions.

The bottom line is that if you want good security, you must use NTFS rather than FAT. NTFS not only offers a much finer level of control over what users can do with a folder or file from across the network, but also offers protection from users with local accounts. For example, a user can't get access to folders or files on the local computer even if he has a local account, unless the permissions on those folders and files have been specifically set to give him access.

Simple File Sharing

Windows XP Professional and Windows XP Home Edition both provide resource sharing. By default, both use a feature called Simple File Sharing (SFS), which Microsoft designed to make it easier to share folders and files. For a detailed explanation of SFS, see `http://support.microsoft.com/default.aspx?scid=kb;en-us;304040`.

When SFS is enabled, all access to shared resources is handled through the Guest account. So, you must enable the Guest account in the **Local Users and Groups** console to allow sharing. In addition, Windows creates a Shared Documents folder that you can use to share documents. Just drag the document to the folder to make it available to others on the network.

With SFS turned off, you have much greater control over who can access folders and files and what actions they can perform with them. When SFS is off, Windows uses the account supplied by the remote user to determine access permissions. You must configure permissions on folders and files to control access.

Which is best? In a small or home network where security is not a major issue, SFS can certainly simplify sharing. When security is a consideration—such as when you need to prevent access by certain users or give different levels of access to different users—you must turn off SFS and use NTFS permissions to control access.

Follow these steps to turn SFS on or off:

1. Open any folder and choose the **Tools**⇨ **Folder Options** menu item.

2. Click the **View** tab, scroll to the bottom of the **Advanced Settings** list, and enable or clear the **Use simple file sharing** check box.

3. Click the **OK** button.

Configuring Folder and File Permissions

Before you share a folder, you should set permissions on the folder to control access to it. The file system must be NTFS to set folder or file permissions.

When SFS is off and the file system is NTFS, you can configure permissions to control access to folders and files on a very granular basis. Before you set permissions, however, create the accounts (and optionally, groups) you will use to allocate permissions. Then, follow these steps to configure the access permissions on a folder or file:

1. Locate the folder or file in Windows Explorer, right-click the folder or file, and choose the **Properties** menu item.

2. Click the **Security** tab (see Figure 8.7).

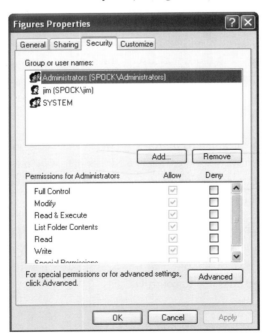

Figure 8.7: Security Tab.

3. If the user or group is not listed in the **Group or user names** box, click the **Add** button to display the **Select Users or Groups** dialog box. Enter the user or group name (or click the **Advanced** button to search for it) and click the **OK** button.

4. Back in the folder properties, click the user or group and then use the check boxes in the **Permissions** area to configure access. Then, click the **OK** button.

Tech Tip:
Click the **Allow** check box to allow the permission for the selected user or group. Click the **Deny** check box to deny that permission to the selected user or group.

Enabling File and Printer Sharing in Windows 98

If the File and Printer Sharing service isn't enabled on the computer from which you want to share resources, you must enable it. Follow these steps on Windows 98 to enable sharing:

1. Right-click **Network Neighborhood** and choose the **Properties** menu item.

2. Click **File and Printer Sharing** on the **Configuration** tab and place a check in both check boxes (see Figure 8.8), then click the **OK** button.

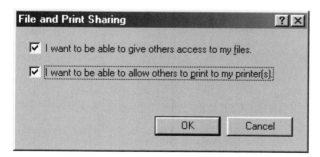

Figure 8.8: File and Print Sharing Dialog Box.

3. Let Windows restart the computer.

File and printer sharing is enabled by default for Windows 2000 and later.

Setting up the Share

With the account(s) created and permissions set, you're ready to start sharing folders. The following sections explain how to do this for various operating systems.

Windows 98 and Me

Follow these steps with Windows 98 and Me to share a folder:

1. Right-click the folder and choose the **Sharing** menu item to open the **Sharing** tab (as shown in Figure 8.9).

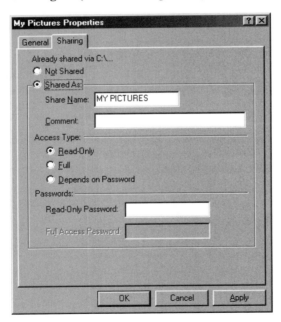

Figure 8.9: Sharing Tab in Windows 98 and Millenium Edition.

2. Change the share name, if desired.

3. From the **Access Type** group, choose one of the following permissions:

▶ **Read-Only** — Remote users can read the contents but not modify them.

▶ **Full** — Remote users can read, modify, and delete folders and files.

▶ **Depends on Password** — Use this option to allow both read-only and full access to the share depending on the password the remote user provides. Enter a unique password for each type of access in the **Passwords** group.

4.   Click the **OK** button to start sharing the folder.

Windows 2000, XP, and 2003

In Windows 2000, Windows XP, and Windows 2003, the dialog boxes look slightly different, but the process is the same for sharing folders. The following steps use Windows XP as an example:

1.   Right-click the folder and choose **Sharing and Security** to display the **Sharing** tab (see Figure 8.10).

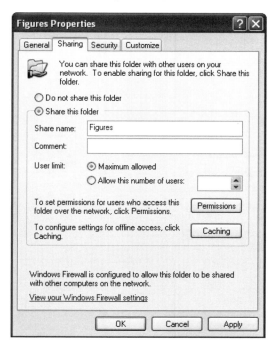

Figure 8.10: Sharing Tab in Windows 2000, XP, 2003.

2. Select the option **Share this folder**, then (if desired) change the share name in the **Share name** field.

3. Click the **Permissions** button to open the **Permissions** dialog box (as shown in Figure 8.11), where you set share permissions.

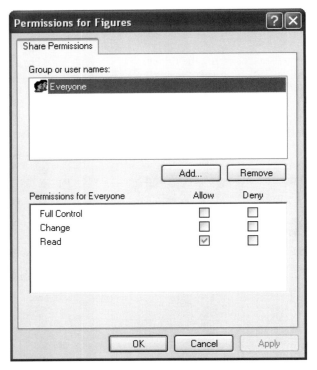

Figure 8.11: Permission Settings for Shared Folder.

4. Place a check in the **Allow** or **Deny** column for each permission to set the desired level and click the **OK** button.

5. Click the **OK** button on the properties for the folder to start sharing the folder.

Note:

Setting share permissions as explained in Step 4 does not set NTFS permissions on the underlying folder. You must use the **Security** tab to configure NTFS permissions. Also note that when permissions conflict, the more restrictive permission takes precedence.

Backup Considerations

ocument backup is an important issue to consider when you're setting up sharing on ur network. If you implement a server-based sharing structure, backups are easy. You n install a backup application such as Iomega Automatic Backup (www.iomega.com) or eritas Backup Exec (www.veritas.com) on the server and back up the shared folder(s) to pe or external disk.

you use peer sharing, backup becomes much more complex. Consider adding an external rd disk to each computer and use automatic backups to ensure that user documents e backed up on a regular basis. Or, choose a network-based backup solution such as ickup Exec that lets the server pull documents from client computers to back them up. nderstand that a bad (or absent) backup and recovery plan can break a business. Take e time to understand the risks of data loss and the importance of a complete backup and saster recovery solution for your business.

Caution:

Whether you back up at the server or at each computer, remember that an office-wide catastrophe can destroy your backup copies as well as the originals. Take critical backup copies offsite to guard against a complete loss.

Sharing Printers

inters are fairly cheap these days, but it's still more cost effective to share a printer with ier users on the LAN. All Windows versions allow you to share a printer.

> **Note:**
> If you haven't enabled File and Printer Sharing in Windows 98/Me, see the section "Enabling File and Printer Sharing in Windows 98" earlier in this chapter for details. Sharing is enabled by default for Windows 2000 and later.

Sharing a Printer in Windows 98/Me

Follow these steps in Windows 98 or Windows Me to share a printer:

1. Open My Computer and open the Printers folder.

2. Right-click the printer and choose the **Sharing** menu item to open the **Sharing** tab.

3. Enter a share name in the **Share Name** field. To optionally password-protect the printer, enter a password in the **Password** field.

4. Click the **OK** button.

Sharing a Printer in Windows 2000/XP/2003

Follow these steps to share a printer in Windows 2000, Windows XP, or Windows 2003

1. Open the Printers and Faxes folder from the Control Panel.

2. Right-click the printer and choose the **Sharing** menu item to open the **Sharing** tab.

3. Choose the option **Share this printer** and enter a share name in the **Share name** field.

4. If other computers on the LAN that will print to this printer use different operating systems, click the **Additional Drivers** button to open the **Additional Drivers** dialog box.

5. Place a check beside the additional drivers you want to copy to the local computer. If a listed client connects to the computer to print and doesn't already have the print driver installed, the computer can download and

install the driver from the sharing computer.

6. Click the **OK** button to close the **Add Drivers** dialog box, then click the **OK** button to close the printer properties and begin sharing the printer.

sing a Separator Page

a printer is very active, it's a good idea to separate print jobs so that users can easily entify their jobs from other users' jobs. When separator pages are enabled, Windows ints a special page between each print job to identify the document owner and other formation.

llow these steps to enable separator pages:

1. Right-click the printer and choose the **Properties** menu item.

2. Click the **Advanced** tab, and then click the **Separator Page** button to open the **Separator Page** dialog box.

3. Click the **Browse** button to choose a separator page, and then click the **Open** button.

4. Click the **OK** button to apply the change, and then click the **OK** button to close the printer properties.

ntrolling Printer Access

Windows 2000 or later you can configure permissions to control what tasks, if any, a user group can perform with a printer. Follow these steps to configure printer security:

1. Right-click the printer and choose the **Properties** menu item, then click the **Security** tab.

2. Click a user or group to view the current permissions, then set or clear the check for the print permissions as needed.

3. Click the **OK** button to apply the change.

Summary

Sharing folders, files, and printers is probably the most common reason for installing a network. Sharing a broadband connection comes in a close second. When setting up sharing, you can set up a dedicated server, use peer-to-peer sharing, or a combination of the two.

Whatever type of sharing you use on your network, security is an important consideration for most networks. Make sure you take security into account to ensure that users can only access the folders, files, and printers they are authorized to use.

Also take backups into account. It's often easier to implement a backup solution if documents are stored on a server, but several solutions are available to help you back up all computers on the LAN.

Chapter 9

Adding Wireless to the Mix

Nothing adds convenience to a network like wireless access. But few things add more security risk. Integrating wireless in your network can be a good thing...as long as you take the time to do it right.

This chapter explores wireless solutions and how to integrate them in your network. In addition to covering wireless technology selection, this chapter also explains how to install a wireless access point, configure the wireless network for security, and integrate your wireless and wired segments.

Let's get started with a look at the wireless solutions you might choose.

Choosing a Wireless Solution

As when choosing wired network components, you have several issues to consider when choosing a wireless solution. The following sections explain these issues.

Speed

A slow network might be useful, but not very. Even if wireless access is more a luxury than a necessity for your network, you should still look to maximize speed.

There are three common wireless options available today:

► **802.11a** — This standard supports up to 54Mbps and operates in the uncrowded 5GHz band. Typical range is from 25-75 feet indoors. Public hotspots are generally unavailable.

▶ **802.11b** — This standard provides for up to 11Mbps data rates and is readily available. Many public hotspots support 802.11a. It operates in the relatively crowded 2.4GHz band with cordless phones and certain other devices. Typical range is from 100-150 feet indoors.

▶ **802.11g** — This standard supports up to 54Mbps and operates in the 2.4GHz band. It is backward compatible with 802.11b at 11Mbps, and G-band public hotspots are becoming much more common. It is not compatible with 802.11a.

802.11g has seen a lot of growth and has quickly become the wireless option of choice 802.11b is somewhat less expensive, but the relatively low cost for 802.11g access point and other hardware make 802.11g my recommended solution. Not only does 802.11 offer the best speeds, but newer versions of the technology have doubled the speed t a theoretical 108Mbps, roughly on par with a 100Mbps wired network, although actua speeds are generally lower.

Range

As the bulleted list in the previous section indicates, range varies from 25 to 150 fee depending on the standard used and other factors. The building's construction has a bi impact on wireless range. Buildings with lots of metal infrastructure and concrete wi have shorter range.

If you believe that range might be problem, look for a range extender when you purchas your wireless access point. Range extenders can take the form of a replacement antenn an auxiliary antenna, or a separate device. These act as repeaters.

Note:

WAP placement has a big impact on range. See "Physical Installation," later in this chapter for details.

ompatibility

he previous section on wireless technology speed included a list of the three main ireless technologies available today. If you have no wireless devices in place now, ompatibility is not a real issue. You can choose a standard based on whatever criteria you ant, then simply make sure all wireless devices you buy in the future are compatible. ltimately, I believe this means buying either 802.11b or 802.11g. I don't see 802.11a king off. My advice is to go with 802.11g. Any 802.11b devices you obtain later (if any) ill be compatible, and most new devices will likely support 802.11g.

river Support

your computers are running Windows XP, you should have few problems integrating ireless components into your network. If not, you need to carefully consider the drivers ovided with the wireless adapters (drivers are not an issue for access points, as they ve their own built-in operating system). Make sure the devices you are planning to buy clude driver support for all of the operating systems under which you'll use them.

nstalling a Wireless Access Point

hen you've picked out the wireless components, it's time to set them up and start joying the benefits of wireless connectivity.

hysical Installation

e first step in setting up a wireless network is to install and configure the wireless cess point. The first decision is where the WAP will be located. Here are a few points consider:

▶ **Location for range and access** — Placement of the access point will determine whether it will cover all of the devices that need access. A central location is probably the best, although you might have to adjust the location because of structure considerations. For example, if you're trying to cover two buildings, you might need to place the WAP near a window or on a wall facing the other building. Also, keep access points away from heavy powered areas, microwave ovens, and wireless phone base stations.

▶ **Wired connection** — Unless you have no wired devices and no Internet connection to share, the WAP will need to be connected by wire to the LAN. This doesn't mean that the WAP must be near the switch or broadband connection. You can run as much as a 100-meter cable to the WAP (assuming Cat5e or better).

▶ **Security** — Physical security is another consideration for the WAP. Place it in a location where it can't be bumped, disconnected, or otherwise abused by people who shouldn't touch it.

Most WAPs can simply sit on a desk or shelf. If you prefer, you can mount the WAP on wall.

WAP Configuration

Each WAP provides a different configuration interface, but most share a common set properties that must be set. Most manufacturers use a Web-based interface to configure th WAP. Figure 9.1 shows the configuration interface for a LinkSys WRT54AG broadban router/wireless access point.

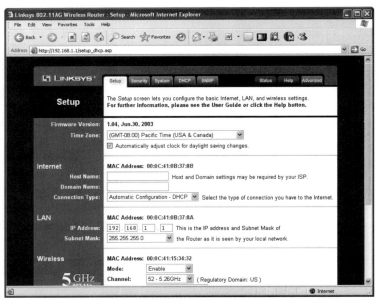

Figure 9.1: WAP Configuration Interface.

Here are the common configuration properties to be set in the WAP:

▶ **LAN IP address / subnet mask** — This address will serve as the gateway for wireless devices. A good practice is to use the first IP address in the subnet assigned to the wireless segment, such as 192.168.1.1.

▶ **WAN IP address / subnet mask** — If the WAP is functioning as a broadband router, this address is either assigned to you by your ISP or is taken dynamically from the ISP's DHCP server. If the WAP is connected to a wired LAN, use a unique address assigned from the LAN's subnet.

▶ **SSID** — The Service Set Identifier (SSID), up to 32 characters in length, uniquely identifies the WAP to wireless clients.

▶ **SSID broadcast** — Enable SSID broadcast to enable wireless clients to automatically detect the wireless LAN. Disable SSID broadcast to hide the wireless LAN for greater security.

▶ **WEP** — Wired Equivalent Privacy (WEP) uses encryption to protect wireless data. Encrypting the data stream minimizes the chance that data can be sniffed and stolen. You should enable WEP, particularly if you do online banking or other sensitive transactions on your wireless LAN.

▶ **WEP encryption** — Specifies the level of encryption for WEP and can be 40, 64, 128, or 152 bits. The higher the number of bits, the greater the security. The tradeoff is performance.

▶ **WPA** — Wi-Fi Protect Access (WPA) is a successor to WEP that provides better security. If your access point supports WPA, you should enable it.

▶ **Passphrase** — Many devices prompt you for a passphrase and then use that passphrase to generate the keys used for WEP encryption.

▶ **Key(s)** — You either enter these keys manually or allow the device to create them from a specified passphrase. The key must be provided by each wireless client, so you must enter a key in the wireless interface properties on each client device or use a method such as the Windows XP Wireless Setup Wizard to specify the key automatically.

▶ **Remote management** — Enable remote management if you want to be able to manage the WAP from its WAN interface. Otherwise, the WAP can only be managed from the LAN side. You must also specify a remote management port and ensure that this port is open in the firewall and (if needed) is port-fowarded to the WAP.

▶ **Authentication type** — Choose between Open System and Shared Key. In an open system, the client and WAP do not use a shared key for authentication. In shared key mode, the WAP and client exchange a WEP key for authentication.

Naturally, the WAP will offer a broad range of other settings that are not really specif to wireless access. For example, the WAP might support DHCP for automatic addres assignment to clients, and require that you configure DHCP settings.

Routing and Traffic Flow Between Wired and Wireless Segments

When the WAP sits on a LAN and acts as a gateway between a wireless segment and wired segment, routing and traffic flow between the two networks can be an issue. Tw situations deserve mention:

▶ **Wireless clients browse the wired LAN and need Internet access** — In this scenario, the wired clients do not need to access the wired clients for file access or printing. Configuration is easy—just configure the WAP as a router/gateway between the two segments. The WAP will provide all necessary routing and port management to enable wireless clients access to the LAN as well as the Internet.

▶ **Wired clients must be able to browse wireless clients** — When wired computers need to access folders or printers on wireless clients, the configuration becomes more complex. Not only do the wired clients need to know how to get their traffic to the wireless side, but the WAP's firewall, if present, must be disabled or configured with port forwarding to enable traffic to flow to the target clients. You can configure some access points in bridge mode to enable unfettered access between wired and wireless segments.

Typical Configuration

,et's assume a typical configuration for the wired/wireless network. Figure 9.2 illustrates uch a configuration.

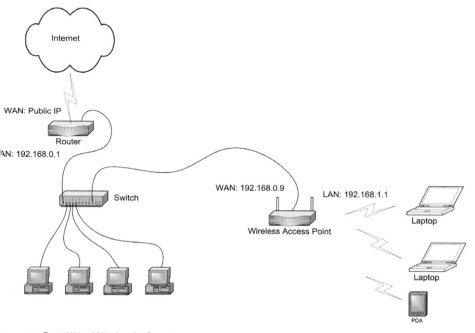

gure 9.2: Typical Wired/Wireless Configuration.

ı Figure 9.2, the wired segment resides on the subnet 192.168.0.n and the wireless segment :sides on 192.168.1.n. The broadband router at 192.168.0.1 serves as the Internet gateway ır the network, and the WAP at address 192.168.1.1 serves as the gateway for the wireless AN. The WAP's address on the wired LAN is 192.168.0.9.

ı this configuration, wireless clients do not need to "know" how to forward traffic to ıe 192.168.0.n subnet because the WAP lives on that subnet and will forward traffic ıtomatically. However, the wired clients do need to know how to forward traffic to the)2.168.1.n subnet because their default gateway—the broadband router—does not live ı that network.

Note:

Routing to the wireless LAN is only needed if the wired clients need to access resources in the wireless LAN.

You can take one of two approaches to the problem:

▶ **Add a route in the wired LAN router/firewall** — In this approach, you add a route in the wired network's gateway that points to the LAN interface of the WAP. Using the subnet examples described previously, the destination for the route would be 192.168.1.0 with a mask of 255.255.255.0, and the gateway for the route would be 192.168.0.9. This method offers the advantage of centralized configuration and creation of a single route.

▶ **Add routes to the wired clients** — An alternative is to add a route on each wired client that needs access to wireless resources. You can use the **ROUTE** command, discussed in Bonus Chapter 11, to add the route:

```
ROUTE -P ADD 192.168.1.0 MASK 255.255.0 192.168.0.9
METRIC 2
```

Note:

The -P switch makes the route permanent. If you omit the switch, you must add the route every time you reboot a client, either manually or through a logon or startup script.

Adding the route is one part of the routing solution. You must also configure the WAP allow the traffic to come in. In some situations, simply turning off the WAP's firewall is workable solution if you're not concerned about traffic flow from the LAN to the WLAN If only one computer on the WLAN needs to be accessed by wired clients, an alternative is to use port forwarding to forward TCP port 445 to the target server on the WLAN. you are using Windows 9x or Me clients, you must also open UDP ports 137 and 138, an TCP port 139. Finally, if the WAP's firewall allows you to do so, you can simply ope these ports.

Caution:

It's unwise to open these ports on a router that sits on the Internet as it opens your network to all sorts of security risks, including certain worms that propagate through those ports.

Configuring Client Access between Segments

Chapter 8 explained how to set up folder and printer sharing. When you're working through a WAP or other router to get to another network segment, you have to do things a bit differently, because in most cases NetBIOS will not work through the WAP. For later clients like Windows XP, NetBIOS is not enabled. NetBIOS is part of the mechanism that enables computers to browse for resources by computer name.

When you need to map to a folder across the WAP, specify the IP address rather than the host name. For example, assume you are working from a computer on the wired side at 192.168.0.100 and need to get to a folder shared by a wireless computer at 192.168.1.200. Assuming the folder is shared as Documents, the UNC path to it would be \\192.168.1.200\Documents.

If too many computers on the segment translates into too many IP addresses to remember, you can add the host-to-address mapping in the hosts file, located in \Windows\System32\drivers\etc.

Securing Your Wireless Network

It is very difficult for a hacker to get into a wired network if it is protected from the Internet by even a rudimentary firewall that performs NAT. If that hacker has physical access to the network, however, your security is completely blown. Because WLANs use radio waves for their transport medium, wireless networks are much more susceptible to compromise. As a trip to www.worldwidewardrive.org will show you, a great many wireless LANs are improperly configured from a security standpoint and are wide open to hackers.

By configuring a handful of settings for your WLAN, you can lock it down to make it safe and secure. Read on to learn how.

SSIDs and Security

The Service Set Identifier (SSID) identifies the WLAN to wireless clients. By default most WAPs broadcast their SSIDs to make it easy for wireless clients to locate wireless networks. That's why when you boot a Windows XP computer with a wireless interface Windows XP can automatically connect to whatever wireless network it finds without any help from you.

One step you can take to reduce (but not eliminate) unauthorized access to your WLAN is to turn off SSID broadcast. Doing so prevents the WAP from broadcasting its SSID, in effect hiding it from wireless clients that don't know it's there. However, it's still possible to sniff out a wireless network with the right tools. So, turning off SSID broadcast is just one step.

Note:

You can rename the SSID to something difficult to guess, as well as turn off broadcast, to prevent unauthorized access.

WEP, WPA, and Other Security Mechanisms

The most important step for securing a WLAN is to implement encryption and authentication. You might think that enabling WEP, even with a 128-bit encryption key, would provide great security. However, a hacker can typically crack even a 128-bit key within a couple of weeks. To address this problem, you should change WEP keys at least every week. Doing so, however, introduces a level of administrative overhead that many small network administrators don't want to bother with.

For this reason, it's important to choose a WAP that supports WPA. Why is WPA more secure than WEP? First, WPA supports a 256-bit encryption key, which are exponentially more difficult to crack than 128-bit keys. The real benefit, however, is that unlike WEP keys, WPA keys are dynamic—they change automatically at whatever interval you have set. For example, the Linksys default WPA interval is 50 minutes. By changing keys frequently and using a larger encryption key, WPA makes it extremely difficult to crack the key.

f your WAP does not support WPA, make sure to change the WEP encryption keys requently. You can use the Windows XP Wireless Setup Wizard to simplify the task for Vindows XP clients.

onfiguring Wireless Clients

Vith the WAP in place and configured, you're ready to configure wireless clients. As inted at previously, Windows XP makes the process almost painless by enabling clients o automatically locate and connect to wireless networks. However, this assumes that the VLAN is either configured for Open mode without WEP/WPA, or you have used the Vireless Network Setup Wizard or other method to deploy the keys and other settings to lients. This Wizard lets you store the required wireless settings to a USB flash drive or iskette for distribution to other clients.

Jsing the Windows XP Wireless Network Setup Wizard

ollow these steps to use the Wireless Network Setup Wizard:

1. Connect a wireless client adapter to the computer.

2. Open the Network Connections folder from the Control Panel and click on the wireless interface.

3. In the left pane, click **View Available Wireless Networks**.

4. In the **Wireless Network Connection** window (see Figure 9.3), click **Set up a wireless network for a home or small office**.

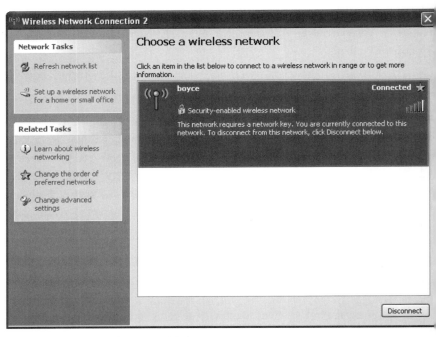

Figure 9.3: Wireless Network Connection Window.

5. When the wizard starts, click the **Next** button. The wizard prompts for several items, such as SSID, WPA/WEP settings, and so on. Provide the settings required by the wizard.

6. When the wizard is finished, you can specify that it copy the settings to a USB flash drive or other drive, or print the settings to use for manual configuration.

7. To configure a computer using the USB drive or other disk created by the wizard, run the wizard on the target computer. Choose the option to add new computers to the WLAN and click the Next button.

8. Specify the path to the disk and follow the remaining wizard prompts to complete the setup.

Windows XP Manual Configuration

If you do not want to use automatic configuration for your wireless network because you want to lock down security, you must manually configure wireless settings on the client. Use the following steps to configure wireless access. This section assumes you are using Windows XP as the client. Configuration of other clients is similar.

1. Connect the wireless device to the computer, then open the Network Connections folder.

2. Right-click the wireless interface and choose **Properties**, then click the **Wireless Networks** tab (see Figure 9.4).

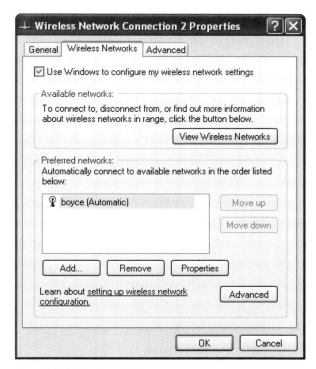

Figure 9.4: Wireless Networks Tab.

3. If the WLAN appears in the **Preferred networks** list, click the WLAN and click the **Properties** button. Otherwise, click the **Add** button to create a new connection.

4. Click the **Association** tab.

5. On the **Association** tab, enter the SSID, authentication type, encryption type, keys, and other information based on the following list:

    ▶ **Network name** — Enter the WLAN's SSID in this field.

    ▶ **Network authentication** — Choose between **Open** and **Shared**, depending on the authentication type used by the WLAN.

    ▶ **Data encryption** — Choose the encryption method used by the WLAN (or choose Disabled if encryption is not used).

    ▶ **Network key** — Enter a valid network key for the WLAN.

    ▶ **Confirm network key** — Re-enter the network key to confirm it.

    ▶ **Key index** — Specify the key index. For example, if the WAP offers four encryption keys and you use the last key in the list, choose key index **4**.

    ▶ **The key is provided for me automatically** — Choose this option if the key is provided automatically, such as in a preconfigured wireless adapter.

    ▶ **This is a computer-to-computer (ad hoc) network** — Choose this option if you are setting up an ad hoc WLAN with no WAP.

6. Click the **Authentication** tab.

7. Configure settings on the **Authentication** tab according to the following list:

    ▶ **Enable IEEE 802.1x authentication for this network** — Choose this option to use authentication from a certificate, such as from a smart card or one installed on the client computer.

    ▶ **EAP type** — Choose between **Protected EAP** and **Smart Card or Other Certificate**, depending on the source of the certificate.

▶ **Authenticate as computer when computer information is available** — Enable this option if you want the client to be able to authenticate to the WLAN when no user is logged on to the computer.

▶ **Authenticate as guest when user or computer information is unavailable** — Enable this option if you want the client to attempt to authenticate on the WLAN if no user or computer information is available.

8. Click the **Connection** tab.

9. Enable the option **Connect when this network is in range** if you want Windows to automatically connect to the WLAN when it comes into range. Disable the option if you want to manually initiate a connection from the Network Connections folder.

Configuration for Other Operating Systems

Windows XP and Windows 2003 provide built-in wireless support, but previous versions of Windows do not. Using wireless adapters in these older operating systems requires installing vendor-supplied drivers and configuration software. The configuration software varies by vendor, so check the manual to determine how to run the configuration utility and configure the card according to the settings required by the WLAN.

Summary

Choosing wireless LAN hardware isn't really difficult. If you need to provide compatibility with older devices or computers with built-in wireless hardware, choose a solution that provides the best speed while remaining compatible with the older devices. If you have no WLAN hardware currently, choose a fast G-band device. Look for one that supports WPA as well as WEP for best security.

If range proves to be a problem, you should be able to add a range extender to your network with a replacement antenna or range extender. In some situations, adding an external antenna to the client will enable it to connect to a remote WAP.

Physical security for the WAP is important when setting up a WLAN, but configuring and using security on the WLAN is even more important. If your WAP and clients support WPA, enable and use WPA. Use WEP for those WAPs and client cards that do not support WPA and make sure to change the WEP keys at least once a week.

Chapter 10

Using Voice Over IP

Not too many years ago, Internet use was limited primarily to Web browsing and e-mail. As the infrastructure broadened to provide more bandwidth and broadband became more commonly available, the Internet became a means to deliver other types of data.

One of the many interesting developments in technology related to the Internet in recent years is *Voice over IP*, otherwise known as VoIP. This technology enables you to conduct phone calls over a broadband Internet connection, even with others who don't have VoIP.

This chapter explores these topics to give you a better understanding of them and help you implement some of these technologies in your own network.

Using VoIP

Despite jokes to the contrary, the POTS (Plain Old Telephone System) works very well and provides a reliable means for you to contact anyone in the world with a phone. Why then would you want to add something new like VoIP to the mix?

The main reason is cost. An overseas call often costs many times per minute what a long distance call within your own country costs. In addition, each long distance call you make with your traditional phone provider is typically charged a per-minute rate, regardless of how many calls you make—each one costs money.

Because of telecommunications deregulation, Internet Service Providers and other companies can now offer voice services over the Internet. The cost model is different from current, traditional POTS models. Plans vary by provider (and many providers offer several plans), but in general, you pay a monthly flat fee for unlimited calls rather than pay a per-minute charge for every non-local call you make.

For example, Vonage (www.vonage.com) currently offers a plan for $25.99US that provides unlimited calls within the US and Canada, as well as several other services such as voice mail, caller ID, call waiting, three-way calling, and more. You can also make international calls at a fixed rate per minute that varies by country. Vonage's service also provides free calls between Vonage users. So, cutting telecommunications costs is one of the main reasons for using a VoIP solution.

Another benefit to using VoIP is the capability to choose an area code in almost any location. Many VoIP providers let you specify a non-local area code for an additional monthly fee. This feature lets people in the target area code call you for the cost of a local call, even if they don't have VoIP.

Many providers also offer virtual phone numbers, enabling you to have a phone presence in more than one location. For example, if your company is based on the east coast, you can add a virtual number in a west coast state to provide a virtual presence there for your company. This virtual presence not only gives your customers the idea that you are local to their area, but enables them to call a local number to contact you.

VoIP offers many other useful features (some of these are specific to certain providers):

▶ **Voicemail** — Like many cellular providers, most VoIP providers offer the capability to record voice messages and even forward them to your Inbox via e-mail, where you can receive them while away from your phone.

▶ **Call Logs** — You can maintain an electronic call log on your computer to keep track of when calls were made and to whom, and quickly start a new call to a previous number with a mouse click.

▶ **Phone Book** — You can store names and numbers in an electronic phone book for quick and easy access and automated dialing.

▶ **Locate Me / Ring List** — You can configure your service to forward calls to other numbers when you are not at your primary phone, specify multiple alternate numbers, and even have all of them ring at the same time.

▶ **Do Not Disturb** — You can selectively receive calls, forwarding non-urgent calls to voicemail.

▶ **Call Filtering** — You can specify who may or may not call you. Calls can be blocked or forwarded to voicemail.

▶ **Conference Calling** — You can set up and conduct a call with multiple parties.

▶ **Record and Send** — You can record a voice message and send it to multiple recipients without the need to make multiple calls.

▶ **International Call Block** — You can prevent unauthorized users from placing international calls by blocking those calls. Authorized users can continue to make international calls.

▶ **Call Hunt** — If you have multiple numbers on the same account, you can use this feature to forward incoming calls to other numbers so you don't miss important calls. You can specify the call hunt sequence.

▶ **Number Portability** — With this feature, you can carry your VoIP network adapter with you and continue to make and receive calls at the same number, regardless of where you are.

▶ **Repeat Dialing** — If a number is busy, you can have your computer dial the number repeatedly until it rings, then ring your own phone.

▶ **Toll Free Calls** — You can enable customers, family, and friends to call you at no charge to them. The toll charge is billed to you at a relatively low rate comparable to regular long distance charges.

As useful as it is, VoIP does have a few drawbacks. First, VoIP requires power for the VoIP equipment as well as the broadband equipment. If a power failure occurs and this equipment isn't protected by a UPS, you'll lose your VoIP service. You also need a fast, reliable broadband connection to make and receive calls. In addition, 911 emergency calls will not necessarily work through your VoIP provider without some additional setup.

How VoIP Works

VoIP traffic runs over your existing broadband connection and therefore requires some means to convert voice to digital signals that can be broadcast across the Internet and then reassembled back into voice at the other end.

In a home or small office environment, one solution is to use an adapter (an Analog Telephone Adapter, or ATA) that plugs in between a regular analog phone and the Internet. The adapter translates calls to and from digital signals that can be transmitted across the network. Some adapters connect directly to the network, and others connect to your computer. Some VoIP providers also offer software-based calling in which you use a program installed on your computer, along with a computer headset and microphone to place and receive calls.

In situations where you need to provide VoIP capabilities to everyone in the office, an alternative to individual adapters is to install a VoIP-capable Private Branch Exchange (PBX). The PBX then supports outgoing calls both over the POTS and through IP. Such a setup enables you to easily provide VoIP throughout the entire office and gives you the capabilities of a typical PBX, such as hold, paging, forwarding, music on hold, and so on.

Quality of Service

Because VoIP relies on a broadband connection, the quality of service and overall bandwidth available to you will affect your VoIP service and call quality. Naturally, the higher your available bandwidth, the better your experience with VoIP will be. You can improve call quality by limiting the other activities you perform on the network while placing a call, such as stopping any streaming audio or video. However, a better approach is to ensure that you have enough bandwidth to accommodate all of your Internet needs.

Upstream speed of your connection determines how fast data is sent out of your network to the Internet. Downstream speed determines how fast data is received. If you don't currently know what your upstream and downstream speeds are, check with your ISP. You might also want to perform a speed test for your connection to determine its capabilities. You'll find several options for testing your connection at http://tech.msn.com/products/ speedtest.armx. Vonage offers a speed test link at www.vonage.com/help _ broadband.php . A search at any popular Internet search site on the term "broadband speed test" will turn up other test sites.

o, how much bandwidth is enough? Two major providers, Vonage and AT&T, both recommend at least 90Kbps or better in both directions for highest quality audio. Naturally, a higher bandwidth will give you more room for other tasks such as Web browsing, streaming audio and video, file downloads, and other tasks while using your internet phone service.

Planning a VoIP Installation

Installing VoIP capability for a single computer on your network is a relatively easy process. However, even in a single-phone installation, you still need to consider a handful of issues.

Note:

Because there are many VoIP equipment vendors, providers, and installation scenarios, this section does not cover installation specifics. Rather, it explores common VoIP planning and installation issues. Consult your provider's Web site for additional information on installing and configuring your VoIP equipment.

Service Options and Topology

First, are you replacing your existing POTS phone system with VoIP? If so, you no longer need your existing phone for telephone calls (unless you want to have two methods for placing calls). However, you still need your existing phone if you have DSL service, which piggybacks on your POTS phone line. So, what do you do if you have DSL?

You have two options. The first is to maintain your existing phone service for DSL and obtain a new number for your VoIP service. If you find two phone numbers and services a hassle, you can switch to a cable Internet connection if your cable provider offers it. This latter approach enables you to transfer your existing phone number to your new VoIP provider so people can continue to call you at your existing number. However, keep in mind that VoIP will then be your *only* means of placing and receiving calls. If the power fails, your phone system will be out until it comes back on. What's more, phone service availability will be subject to Internet availability. If your ISP's circuit goes down, so will your VoIP service.

After you disconnect the line, test to verify that the line is disconnected. Inside th building, pick up a phone that is connected to a jack that previously worked. You shoul hear no sound at all from the phone. If you do, make sure you disconnected the corre cables. If you still hear tone of any kind on the phone, have your phone company make service call to disconnect the lines for you.

Placing the Adapter

Where you locate the VoIP adapter depends on how many phones and computers it wi serve. If the adapter is located between the broadband modem and the internal router (se Figure 10.1), the adapter can prioritize VoIP traffic to ensure a higher quality of servic for voice calls. In effect, the adapter places a higher priority on VoIP traffic than on othe traffic and routes it accordingly.

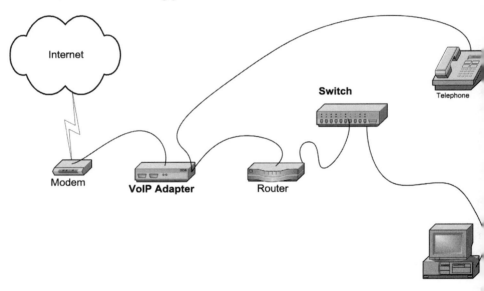

Figure 10.1: VoIP Adapter Prioritizes Voice Traffic.

If your network firewall or router can prioritize VoIP traffic on its own, you can conne the VoIP adapter after the firewall or router, as shown in Figure 10.2. You can also us this setup if you are not concerned about quality of service because you have sufficie bandwidth to accommodate all services on the network concurrently.

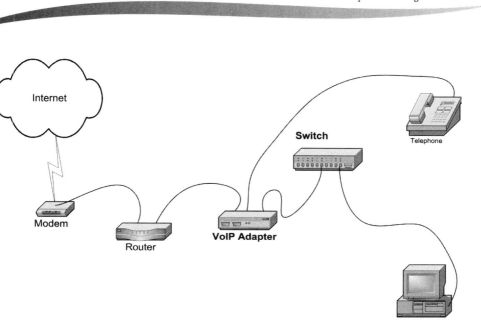

igure 10.2: VoIP Adapter Cannot Prioritize Voice Traffic.

f you want to install more than one phone on the network, you'll need more than one dapter. These adapters are connected to the network after the router.

dapter and Firewall Configuration

ike any other device on the network, the VoIP adapter requires some configuration. For xample, you must specify how it receives its IP address and configure other settings such s DNS servers. If the VoIP adapter sits between your broadband modem and router, the dapter must be configured with the addressing scheme and other settings required by the rovider. For example, if your broadband provider requires you to use PPPoE, you must onfigure the adapter for PPPoE. Generally, you accomplish adapter configuration through Web interface, but check with the adapter documentation and your VoIP provider's upport site for additional information.

fter you configure the adapter, you also need to consider firewall configuration to upport VoIP. Depending on the firewall design, you might need to open specific ports in he firewall to allow VoIP traffic. These ports include the following:

▶ 5060 through 5063 UDP

▶ 123 UDP

► 69 UDP

► 53 UDP

► 10,000 through 20,000 UDP

Ports 123, 69, and 53 should be allowed to the adapter. Ports 5060-5061 and 10,000-20,000 must be port-forwarded in the network's firewall to the internal IP address of the VoIP adapter (assuming it sits behind the firewall or router). If the VoIP adapter is configured to take its address dynamically through DHCP, there is a chance that the adapter's address will change. If so, you'll have to change the port forwarding settings of the adapter accordingly. Configuring the adapter for a static IP avoids this problem, but make sure to exclude the static IP from any DHCP scope on your network to avoid address conflicts.

Ensuring 911 Availability

The 911 emergency system relies on emergency service providers being able to associate your phone number with a physical location. Because the phone number for your VoIP service might be in another area code, ensuring 911 availability requires some additional steps.

Some providers do not offer 911 dialing, although legislation is pending to mandate 911 service for VoIP. Others currently enable it by default, while still others turn it on only if you request it. If you do want to ensure 911 availability for your VoIP service, you need to coordinate with your VoIP provider. Specifically, you must give your provider the physical address where the VoIP adapter is located to enable the provider to properly route 911 calls to emergency services in your area.

If you move and take your VoIP service with you, you must contact the service provider to inform them of the new address. If you move your VoIP adapter temporarily, such as taking it on a business trip or on vacation, you must use another phone to dial 911. Using the VoIP service to dial 911 in this case will result in your 911 calls being forwarded to emergency services at your home location, rather than the new location. Alternately, you can inform the provider of your new temporary location and then switch it back when you return home.

The main point in this discussion is that you should not assume that you have working 911 service through your VoIP service provider. Take the time to investigate the 911 requirements and offerings of your provider and set up your 911 service accordingly.

In addition, when you do need to make a 911 call through your VoIP service, you should give your location to the person who answers. With wireline 911 calls, the emergency services personnel often receive your calling address automatically. This is not necessarily the case with VoIP-based 911 calls.

Availability and incoming emergency calls are also a consideration. If your power or internet service goes out, your ability to call 911 goes with it. What's more, if you have call filtering or blocking in place for your VoIP service, emergency personnel might not be able to call you back if needed. Take all of these issues into consideration when planning your VoIP installation.

PBX Installations for Businesses

If your small business currently uses a PBX for distributed call processing and features like hold, music on hold, intercom paging, and call forwarding, installation of VoIP service could become more complex than a simple network installation. If you want to integrate VoIP for all of your existing phones, your PBX must support VoIP. If that's not currently the case, you must either upgrade the existing PBX to support VoIP or replace it with one that does. You must also contract with a VoIP provider. If you don't have anyone on staff with much experience with the PBX or VoIP, perhaps the best approach is to contact your phone provider for assistance. Or, identify the VoIP providers that offer the types of services and plans you want, and discuss your PBX needs with their sales and technical staff.

You can also integrate VoIP without going through the PBX if you only want VoIP capability for a selected number of users. This scenario is essentially the same as the home installation described previously in this chapter. Each person requiring VoIP access must have his own VoIP ATA adapter connected to the network with a separate phone connected to the adapter. This is in addition to the phone that is connected to the PBX system. The network and firewall configuration issues discussed previously for a home installation also apply.

Choosing a Provider

Several hundred VoIP providers exist in the US alone, with many more located outside of the US. There is no magical process for choosing a VoIP provider. Like any service, choosing the right provider means finding one that offers the services you want at the price you're willing to pay. One good source to locate VoIP providers is http://www voipproviderslist.com. Some of the larger providers include Vonage (www.vonage.com) AT&T (www.voip.com), and Lingo (www.lingo.com).

Free VoIP Services

If you'd like to enjoy the benefits of VoIP without paying for it, you'll be happy to know there are free services you can use to talk with other people across the globe. One downside to these free services is that the other person must have the same service. In addition, you can't make calls to regular phones. However, if neither of these is a major drawback for you, a free VoIP service can be a great way to talk for free on the Internet.

One of the most popular free services is Skype (www.skype.com). You can talk for free for an unlimited period of time to other Skype users. The company also offers a paid service called SkypeOut, which lets you connect to ordinary phones to talk to non-Skype users.

Summary

Voice over IP offers some great advantages over POTS, including reduced long distance rates and the potential for features you might not otherwise have, such as conference calling, virtual area codes, and so on.

To implement VoIP, you'll need to install at least one VoIP adapter for your network. Each separate phone requires its own adapter. Or, you can install a VoIP-capable PBX in your office to support multiple phones. In addition, you'll need sufficient bandwidth to use VoIP. Some of the major providers recommend a minimum of 90Kbps in both directions but quality of service will be better with higher bandwidth.

Finally, keep 911 availability in mind when considering VoIP. Some providers enable 911 calling by default, while others require you to activate it. In all cases, you must notify your VoIP carrier of the physical address at which your adapter is located prior to using the 911 service.

Part IV

Extras

Glossary

802.11a

A wireless standard that supports up to 54Mbps and operates in the 5GHz band; typical range is from 25-75 feet indoors.

802.11b

A wireless standard that provides for up to 11Mbps data rates and operates in the 2.4Ghz band; typical range is from 100-150 feet indoors.

802.11g

A wireless standard that supports up to 54Mbps and operates in the 2.4GHz band; backward compatible with 802.11b at 11Mbps; not compatible with 802.11a.

Analog Telephone Adapter (ATA)

Device used to connect a VoIP telephone to a network.

APIPA

Automatic Private IP Addressing, a means for automatically assigning IP addresses when no DHCP server is present.

Asymmetric Digital Subscriber Line (ADSL)

ADSL uses a standard phone line to connect your network to the Internet. The data signal can piggyback on an existing voice line, meaning your telephone and Internet share the same physical phone line.

Bluetooth

A wireless networking standard that supports 10 to 100 meter range.

Broadband

A high-speed connection to the Internet; typically a Digital Subscriber Line (DSL) or cable connection, but can include satellite connections.

Bus topology	All devices in a bus topology are connected to a common cable called the bus or backbone.
Cable	This broadband option piggybacks on your Cable TV connection.
Content Filter	A content filter blocks Web sites based on a variety of criteria, such as adult content, weapons, language, and so on.
Crossover cable	Network cable in which the send and receive pairs are switched; often used to connect a broadband modem to the local network, or to directly connect two computers without an intermediate hub or switch.
DHCP	Dynamic Host Configuration Protocol; a standard protocol used to automatically assign addresses and other IP configuration data.
DNS	Domain Name System, the system by which host names are associated with IP addresses.
Dynamic DNS	A technology by which client systems can request an update of their DNS records on a DNS server.
Frame Relay	This is actually a packet-switching protocol for connecting devices on a wide area network (WAN). Frame relay works over a T1 or fractional T1 line. In the United States, frame relay supports connections from 56Kbps to 1.544Mbps (although frame relay can also support up to T3, or 45Mbps).
Gateway	A device that serves as a connecting device between two networks; in a small network, the term gateway typically refers to the connection between a private network and the Internet.

Hub	A device that connects one or more computers or other devices to a network; typically less expensive than switches but provides lesser performance.
Internet Control Message Protocol (ICMP)	A protocol that enables computers to send and receive status and error information.
ISP	Internet Service Provider.
MAC address	Media Access Control address; the physical address of a device.
Network address translation (NAT)	A method used to translate or map one IP address to another. Commonly used to protect one network from another through one-way translation.
Network Interface Card (NIC) aka Network Adapter	A device installed in or connected to a device (typically a computer) that connects that device to the network.
Next hop	The next intermediate connection in a string of connections.
Node	Any device on the network.
Packet	A collection of data that is transmitted on a network.
Patch panel	Device used to terminate network cable and serve as a connection between those cables and devices (such as a switch or hub).
Peer-to-peer network	A network in which each client computer can share resources with other computers.

Perimeter firewall	A firewall located at the perimeter of the network that protects all devices inside the network.
Port forwarding	Redirecting incoming traffic for a specific external IP address to a specific internal IP address.
Port triggering	Technology by which a client system can cause a port to be opened in the firewall.
Powerline Network	Network that uses electrical wiring as the data transfer media.
Power-over-Ethernet	A system that provides electrical power to devices over an Ethernet network connection.
Private Branch Exchange (PBX)	A device that provides centralized phone switching and other features such as call hold, music on hold, intercom, and others.
Protocol	The method that nodes on the network use to communicate with one another. TCP/IP is today's most commonly used protocol suite.
Ring topology	Devices are connected to one another in a closed loop, with each device connected to two others, forming a ring.
Router	A device that routes network packets from one network segment to another, such as from a private network to the Internet (and vice-versa).
Server	A device, typically a computer, that provides some service (such as file or print sharing) to other devices.
Server-based network	A network in which a server functions as the primary place to share files, printers, and other resources.

Service Set Identifier (SSID)	A unique identifier for a wireless LAN.
SOHO	Small Office / Home Office.
Star topology	Devices are connected by individual cables to a central hub or switch.
Switch	A device that connects one or more computers to a network.
T1 or Fractional T1	A T1 is a dedicated phone line consisting of 24 channels, each of which supports 64Kbps. A full T1 therefore supports 1.544Mbps.
TCP/IP	Transmission Control Protocol/Internet Protocol; the standard protocol used for Internet traffic and most small or home networks.
Topology	The physical or logical shape of a local area network or other communications system.
Tree topology	The tree topology combines star segments with a linear bus.
Virtual Private Network (VPN)	A secure network that connects one computer or network to another network across an unsecured network such as the Internet.
Voice over IP (VoIP)	A technology that supports transmission of telephone calls across the Internet.
Wi-Fi Protected Access (WPA)	A standard protocol designed to enhance wireless security through improved data encryption and authentication.
Wired equivalent privacy (WEP)	A security protocol for wireless local area networks.

Wireless Access Point (WAP)	Device that serves as a communications hub for wireless devices and typically provides connectivity to a wired network (including the Internet).
Workstation	A computer that is used primarily for end-user functions such as running applications; workstations can also perform server functions.

Index

F

FAT 156
fibre optic cable 34
file and printer sharing, enabling 159-163
File Services for Macintosh, see FSM
File Transfer Protocol, see FTP
files, sharing 13
firewall 29-30, 51, 66
    choosing 56-57
    client 107
    configuration 108-109
    in Windows XP 111
    perimeter 105, 107
    software-based 106
    using third-party 119
fractional T1 24, 30, 52
frame relay 25
frame-relay connection 52
FSM 151
FTP 55

G

G standard 60
gateways 51, 94
    dial-up 27
    Internet 26, 28
G-band 35, 59
HTTP 55, 88
hubs and switches 18, 34, 43-46

I

IANA 88
ICF 111-113, 119
ICMP 85, 114-115
ICS 26, 27, 103-104
IGMP 85
Infrastructure 23
Internet Assigned Numbers Authority, see IANA
Internet connection
    configuring 85
    sharing 14
Internet Control Message Protocol, see ICMP
Internet gateways 26, 61
Internet Group Management Protocol, see IGMP
Internet Protocol, see IP
IP 85

IP addresses 53-54, 83, 86-92
    LAN 98
    private 88-89
    public 88-89, 101
    WAN 98
    WAN gateway 98
IPv4 standard 86
ISA/PCI adapter 61

K

KVM switches 48

L

LAN 38, 86, 94, 103, 53-54, 88-89
    setting addresses 97
    speed 32-33
licensing
    client 108
    modes 147
    per-device 148
    per-server 148
    per-user 148

M

managed hub 45

N

NAT 53-56, 88-89, 108
    disabled 109
    static 109
    with dynamic address 109
    with fixed address 109
    with PPPoE 109
NEC 74
NetBEUI 86
network adapters 34, 59, 121-123
network address translation, see NAT
network cables 18
Network Interface Card, see NIC
networks
    Bluetooth 35
    cabling 43-47
    choosing a client 131-134
    choosing components 43
    client/server 19, 20
    clients 121

Notes

Notes

Notes

IMPORTANT NOTICE
REGISTER YOUR BOOK

Bonus Materials

Your book refers to valuable material that complements your learning experience. In order to download these materials you will need to register your book at http://www.rationalpress.com.

This bonus material is available after registration:

▶ Bonus chapters: "Troubleshooting the Network" and "Beyond the Basic Network"

▶ Links to SOHO networking resources

Registering your book

To register your book follow these 7 easy steps:

1. Go to http://www.rationalpress.com.

2. Create an account and login.

3. Click the **My Books** link.

4. Click the **Register New Book** button.

5. Enter the registration number found on the back of the book (Figure A).

6. Confirm registration and view your new book on the virtual bookshelf.

7. Click the spine of the desired book to view the available downloads and resources for the selected book.

Figure A: Back of your book.